Coffee
with the Savior

A Bible Study for Women

By Kristen Myers

CONCORDIA PUBLISHING HOUSE • SAINT LOUIS

To Paul, Sam, Noah,
and all the encouragers
who knew God could do this,
and to our loving almighty God who did.

"The one who calls you is faithful and He will do it."
1 Thessalonians 5:24 (NIV)

Copyright © 2010 Concordia Publishing House

3558 S. Jefferson Avenue, St. Louis, MO 63118-3968

1-800-325-3040 · www.cph.org

Written by Kristen Myers

Manufactured in the United States of America

Table of Contents

Introduction 4

Chapter 1: He Wants to Have Coffee with Me? 8

Chapter 2: Let's Meet for Coffee 22

Chapter 3: So Good to See You 36

Chapter 4: Sorry I Haven't Called More 52

Chapter 5: What's Going On . . . Really Going On? . 69

Chapter 6: Show Me Your Pictures 84

Chapter 7: We'll Have to Do This Again 98

Chapter 8: The Next Cup 112

Parting Thoughts 125

Introduction

Dear reader, have you ever thought about what you want in a best friend? Is it someone who would meet with you every day? No matter what your mood is, this friend would gladly listen and hear your every word; your every thought and concern would be important. Nothing would get in the way of your friend's being there for you. You would be number one, top priority every day. Your best friend would love you without restraint or condition, would always welcome you, and would never turn away.

If a friend like this has ever been your wish, then I welcome you to a place where you can meet Him. Like you, I once longed for connection and companionship with a friend who truly cared about me. I hoped for someone who would accept me and want to be with me. I have that Someone; His name is Jesus. He wants to be your closest friend too.

I grew up knowing who Jesus was. As an infant, I received His forgiveness and eternal seal through Baptism. Starting in middle school, I regularly received Jesus' body and blood in Holy Communion, fully believing His words "Given and shed for you for the forgiveness of sins." However, even with participation in these wonderful, grace-filled Sacraments, I still didn't understand the intimate relationship Jesus hoped to have with me and with you. One day, as I was reading Jeremiah 29:12–13 in the Bible, I realized the relationship described was something I didn't have with God. Here is what I read:

"Then you will call upon Me and come and pray to Me, and I will hear you.

You will seek Me and find Me, when you seek Me with all your heart."

The verses tugged at my heart. I longed to become friends with this Friend who promised I could call upon Him and come to Him whenever I desired. Yet, I didn't know how. Then, in the stillness of a moment, the verse came alive in a new way. The words of Scripture were like a good friend saying to me, "Meet me for coffee. I want to catch up with you. I want to hear about your day and your life. I want to know your joys and your pain. I want to fully be here for you."

As I sat in the quietness and reflected on the words, my heart seemed to shout, *The friend I need is Jesus! I can have the friendship I've been looking for!*

As I read the verses of Jeremiah again, the words God spoke to the Israelites so long ago suddenly became applicable to my life. I could find my friendship with Him by calling on Him, coming to Him, seeking Him—every day—and receiving Him and His love through His Word to me, the Bible. Since the verses from Jeremiah were instructions from God to His people, this meant that I could go directly to God too (Luke 11:1–4, 9–13). I didn't need a mediator or someone else to speak for me. I didn't have to wait. I could share my deepest needs with God and experience fellowship with Him as I followed His command and invitation to pray (Matthew 7:7–8, 11; Luke 18:1). I could approach Him with prayers of praise, confession, request, and thanksgiving. My excitement grew at the possibilities, but I was unsure about what to do next.

I realized at last that I could speak to my Savior the same way I talk with a best friend I meet for coffee. I could begin by praising Him for His presence in my life, just as I thank my friend for her willingness to meet with me. I could apologize for not calling on Him sooner, just as I would tell my friend how sorry I was for not calling her. I could continue by telling Jesus what truly is bothering me, concerning me, and worrying me in my life. After all, I would share these intimate words with my best girlfriend. Then, I could spend time in His Word, which tells me where He has been, what He has been doing, and what His life means for me. My friend might show photographs that would show me the same about her. After all this, I could tell Jesus that I want to meet with Him again, just as I would plan to get together on another day with my friend. Finally, I could follow through on the commitment to meet with my Savior again. When I love a friend, I do the same thing. We promise to see each other again, and we do.

Through this study, I hope you come to see Jesus as your Friend. Together, we will discover the many ways in which we can relate to God—Father, Son, and Holy Spirit. We will see how He shares our burdens (Matthew 11:28–30), forgives our wrongdoing, and redeems us forever (Psalm 103:3–4). We also will learn more about one of God's chosen people, Moses. Studying what Scripture tells us about his life and his conversations with God will teach us even more about how we can respond to the gifts God gives to each of us.

Whether completing this study in a small group or individually, we can do it together, as friends. Each chapter contains true stories about friendship, as well as biblical accounts of Moses' relationship with his true Friend, God. Scripture references are included in the text to help you dig deeper into God's Word. As you will see, each chapter ends with a section called "Let's Meet Now." This section includes seven questions: one that will help you apply the truths of Jeremiah 29:12–13 and six more that will help you apply God's Word to your own life. You will find ample space between questions where you may write your thoughts. You also may want to keep a journal. Feel free to complete the entire section at one sitting or one question per day for a weekly Bible study schedule. Either way, this study is designed to be uniquely yours.

So grab a cup of coffee, a Bible, and a pen. Then, let me welcome you, friend! Welcome to *Coffee with the Savior*.

Kristen Myers

Chapter 1

He Wants to Have Coffee with Me?

"Then you will call upon Me and come and pray to Me,
and I will hear you.
You will seek Me and find Me, when you seek Me
with all your heart."
Jeremiah 29:12–13

I quickly placed my drink on the table, praying I would not drop my infant son. I buckled him into the high chair next to me. Only then, could I sit and take a drink of my ice-cold diet cola. I surveyed the people around me and saw the well-manicured, stylishly dressed women laughing with one another as they sipped their steaming mugs of specialty coffee.

I couldn't help but wonder why I had decided to stop here. Although I needed a break, seeing these other women reminded me all the more of what I did not have—companionship, a friend who wanted me as a friend in return. I wanted someone on whom I could depend twenty-four hours a day, seven days a week. I wanted someone who would fill the loneliest parts of my soul, someone I could be honest and unguarded with and who still loved me anyway. I wanted a best friend.

Sitting in that coffee shop made it all too easy to compare myself to others and see why I did not have that friend. I was wearing gray and blue sweats with banded ankles. The women around me were dressed in velour running suits. I was in need of a trim and a touch-up on my colored-at-home hair. The women around me sported the latest cuts, with naturally blended highlights. With dry, untended hands I held a hungry, crying infant. They held special coffee cups in soft-looking hands with beautifully manicured nails. In that moment, I just wanted to cry. I doubted. They appeared self-assured. They smiled and laughed as if they had no cares in the world. I left the shop thinking I was not worthy and would never enjoy that kind of relationship with a friend. However, God knew I would.

The Reality of Loneliness

I can't imagine that anyone really wants to live a life of loneliness. For many of us, however, there are times when the reality of being alone sets in with an unwelcome ferocity. No matter the cause, we wish for something that can make our overwhelming emptiness disappear. We hope and pray for something or someone to fill us. We yearn for fulfillment. We desire loving and secure relationships that encourage us and make us feel safe. We long to know others whom we can trust at all times.

This innate yearning for relationship is not an accident. God our Father designed us this way. He created us for relationship with Him and with those He places in our lives—our family, friends, and church community.

Who Would Want Me?

"Who would want me for a friend?" Having moved across the country due to her husband's job transfer, Alicia asked the same question. The women she met seemed so put together. They appeared busily engaged in activities and in the community. Alicia felt alone and left out. She dearly missed her friends back home. Desperate for connection with others in a new city, Alicia hoped for a new friend too.

She noticed a woman who lived in the same neighborhood leaving her children's school. Alicia considered asking the woman, whose name she knew was Shannon, to meet for coffee, but her doubts and insecurity caused her to hesitate. But someone had to break the ice, so after a month and a half of hesitation, the two women finally got together at Shannon's home. Nervous and excited, they began talking about themselves and their families. Before the afternoon was over, Alicia and Shannon decided they would definitely get together again.

Now, more than a year later, they are best friends. They even say they are "inseparable." The similarities between them are amazing, from having chosen the same wedding invitations to often showing up at functions with the same shoes or outfit. No longer feeling alone, both Alicia and Shannon agree that God blesses this friendship. Only He could have ordained the precious connection and commonalities they share. Only God could have given this perfect friend to Alicia.

God did some amazing things in Moses' life too.

God-Ordained Plans

Moses found himself in a foreign place. Born a Hebrew, in a land where his people served as slaves to a mighty pharaoh, Moses should not have lived past infancy. The Egyptian king, anxious about the ever-growing population of Hebrew slaves, declared that all Hebrew male babies were to be thrown into the Nile River and drowned.

Moses' mother followed a different plan. Preparing a basket with tar and pitch for waterproofing, she placed her three-month-old baby in the basket and left him on the bank of the Nile. She sent her daughter, Miriam, to watch over the baby. In Exodus 2, we learn that Moses' mother "saw that he was a fine child" (v. 2). Did she hope someone might rescue Moses, or was this her way of letting him go gently? Did she hope to rescue the baby herself after the threat of death had passed?

In the God-ordained turn of events, the daughter of Pharaoh not only rescued but also adopted Moses. She then, unknowingly, hired Moses' own mother to care for and nurse her adopted Hebrew baby. Through God's compassionate and loving hand, Moses continued living in his family's home. Not until he was older did Moses live in the palace of the same king who ordered him and all other Hebrew boys killed. Instead of dying,

Moses grew up learning the ways of the Egyptian palace. This, one could say, was the first of his foreign experiences.

Moses escaped to his second foreign destination after committing murder. He had witnessed the mistreatment of a Hebrew slave by an Egyptian man, took discipline into his own hands, and faced the consequences (Exodus 2:11–15). After Hebrew men openly confronted him about his actions, Moses fled to Midian. While Moses was there, God not only provided a place for Moses to stay, with the family of Jethro (also called "Reuel," which means "friend of God"), but He also provided him a wife and a son. Moses must have thought he had found his new best friend in his wife. Instead, he was getting ready to find an even greater one.

Will You Be My Friend?

"Will you be my friend?" Did you hear these words as a young girl playing at the park or during recess at school? Maybe you asked the same question of the girl next door. What about in high school? Did you initiate a friendship with a girl sitting next to you in class?

As adults, we may not say the words aloud, but we sometimes find ourselves back at the playground looking for a friend. We wish we could laugh and cry and share our thoughts with someone. Many times, we try to reach out for advice or seek answers from others, wondering whom we can trust. We may wish a friend could be available twenty-four hours a day, seven days a week, someone we could call on or call out to whenever we feel the need.

While I believe God created women with a special desire to have friendships with others, I also know He created us specifically for relationship with His Son, Jesus Christ (1 John 4:9). Jesus is available every minute of every day, anytime we need

Him. Before the beginning of time, God ordained this relationship with Him. He knows the plans He has for us (Jeremiah 29:11). He yearns for intimacy with us (John 3:16). God desires to be a part of our daily life. He cannot wait to reveal Himself as ever-present, alive, and active. He will never leave us (Hebrews 13:5). God wants us to consider Him as our best Friend wherever we are in life (1 John 3:16).

Due to our own sinful nature, however, we are incapable of fellowshiping with God on our own (Isaiah 5:15–16; 59:2; Romans 3:23). Our sin separates us from the very thing we need most—Him. In our sinfulness, we are not His friend; we are His enemy. Because God is a perfect and just God, He cannot allow into His presence anything but perfection. As sinful human beings, left on our own we will never be even close to perfect.

For this reason, out of God's great and unfathomable love for each of us, He set forth a plan that would bring us to perfection. Romans 5:8 tells us, "But God shows His love for us in that while we were still sinners, Christ died for us." God designed the redemptive plan of Jesus dying on the cross, rising three days later, and defeating sin and the devil forever (John 3:16). Through this grace alone, God gives us the privilege of being friends with Him and being in His presence, both now and eternally (John 15:15). Through His Word, which is His conversation with us, and the Sacraments, which are His real presence, God's grace and friendship are ours to receive without restraint.

Does God Want Me?

In the past, I would have read the preceding paragraph and thought, *Sure, that may be true for others, but not for me.* I would have laughed at the words written. Don't get me wrong. I understood that God is the Father of Jesus, the Son, who saved me from my sins. However, the idea of His wanting to be *my* daily

Friend seemed ridiculous. I never believed I was special enough to be His friend. I thought Jesus was someone I could call upon when I had trouble or needed a favor. He was more of a long-distance friend, someone I talked to once in a while because I could not afford to talk to Him more.

A few years ago, if someone had asked if I was interested in becoming close friends with Jesus, my response would have been, "I definitely am not qualified to be one of His friends. I am not loving to others all the time. I get cranky, angry, and tired. I act from my own arrogance, pride, and selfishness more times than I can count. I don't enjoy reading the Bible. I fall asleep at night and forget to pray. I don't go to church all the time. I was even a prodigal daughter for a time. God definitely does not want this girl for a friend."

Maybe you have had the same thought: *If He really knew me, would God want me?* Let me reassure you, dear friend, that He does. God knows who you are; He knows your darkest thoughts and ugliest sin. You can't hide from Him! Psalm 139 assures us that God does know us; He has since the beginning of time. And He wants us anyway!

O LORD, You have searched me and known me!

You know when I sit down and when I rise up;
You discern my thoughts from afar.
You search out my path and my lying down
and are acquainted with all my ways.
Even before a word is on my tongue,
behold, O LORD, You know it altogether.
You hem me in, behind and before,

and lay Your hand upon me.

Such knowledge is too wonderful for me;
it is high; I cannot attain it.

In Your book were written, every one of them,
the days that were formed for me,
when as yet there was none of them.

How precious to me are Your thoughts, O God!
How vast is the sum of them!

If I would count them, they are more than the sand.
I awake, and I am still with You.

Psalm 139:1–6, 16–18

God knows us, and He is with us every moment of our lives. We put up the barriers between our Creator and ourselves. Through the weakness of our own flesh, we allow sinful thoughts and actions to build that wall of separation between God and us. We can be thankful that we do not have to live with that barrier. Our heavenly Father solved this problem for us through His perfect plan of redemption for our sin. Through faith in Christ, our sin, the barrier between us and God, is taken down, and an ongoing friendship with Him is put in its place.

Receiving the Invitation

Many of us perceive that friendships "just happen." This may be true sometimes. Most times, however, a relationship begins when people meet through shared circumstances or events, and evolves as they get to know each other's character and opinions. The friendship deepens with a continued desire to connect and be together. If friendship with God is something you want, you may be wondering, "Does it just happen, or do I have to do something?"

Dear friend, as sinful human beings, we cannot choose to become friends with God on our own. "For by grace you have been saved through faith. And this is not your own doing; it is the gift of God, not a result of works, so that no one may boast" (Ephesians 2:8–9). By our nature, we are not able to believe in Jesus or come to Him without the working of the Holy Spirit within us (1 Corinthians 12:3) and without God first drawing us to Him (John 6:44). He calls us into relationship with Him. He invites us to receive God's grace and salvation.

Jesus extends an invitation to each one of us daily to come and to sit with Him, to drink in His presence, to acknowledge the washing and renewal of His baptismal gifts, to receive His righteousness. Just as you accept the invitation from a friend to meet for coffee and distance yourself from your daily grind, you can also acknowledge the call from Jesus and allow the concerns of this world to melt away. Whether you have always believed in Him, recently came to faith in Him, or have questions about how to get started, Jesus is calling you. No matter where you are in the process, the Savior welcomes you with unconditional love.

As you begin this Bible study today, start by asking God for the simple desire to respond to Him—Father, Son, and Holy Spirit. I am not referring to a desire to like church better, to attend worship more often, or to complete a daily ritual of devotion reading. I mean asking for the desire to share a one-on-one connection with the Savior, where you reveal all your joys, frustrations, hopes, and dreams. I mean a desire for an honest friendship, where you look forward to sharing time together every day.

Let's Meet Now

1. This chapter begins with Jeremiah 29:12–13. In these verses, God speaks through the prophet Jeremiah in a letter to the people of Judah. At that time, they were living as exiles in Babylon. God used these words to tell the captives how He would bring them back to their homeland after seventy years of captivity. Jeremiah's words also promised each person a continued intimate relationship with the one true and living God.

   We can use these same words today as instructions for daily friendship with our Savior. Just as a friend would call and ask us to meet for coffee, God calls us through these verses. He invites us into a relationship where He promises He will listen and answer us *always*. He beckons us to meet with Him and to get to know Him better.

   Personalize these verses by putting them into your own words. Then write them here.

2. Open any popular women's magazine, and you will find friendship quizzes and rating charts. "Experts" tell you how to find friendships if you are looking for them or how to strengthen the ones you already have.

Rate your current friendship with the Savior Jesus Christ.

Nonexistent   Seek Him When   Meet with Him   Meet Daily   Meet and Listen
               I Need Something   Somewhat Regularly   throughout the Day

Comment on your rating. What is holding you back, if anything, from delving deeper into a relationship with your Savior? (Lack of time, doubts, shame, fear of what will be required, etc.)

3. Before the world began, God set in motion a plan that involved you. He knew you before you were born and had all your days designed. He also completed His plan to provide you with the redemption all people need in the form of His Son, Jesus Christ (Jeremiah 29:11).

   Study the following verses. After reading them, write your thoughts about what it would be like to have a friend like the one mentioned. Include your feelings and any insights you gain while spending time with your Friend Jesus.

   a. John 3:16

   b. John 15:13

   c. Romans 3:22–24

   d. Ephesians 2:8–9

4. Many of us may think we know the biblical story of Moses because we learned it when we were young. As an adult, I am amazed at how when rereading a passage of Scripture, God willingly reopens the story and makes it relevant to our current lives. Take time to read Exodus 2:1–10. (If you are not familiar with the story of Moses, read Exodus 1 for the background.)

According to Exodus, Moses should have never lived past his birth. Moses was born into a repressive time in Israel's history. The Hebrews, including his family, lived as slaves under the tyranny of the ruler, or pharaoh (likely Thutmose III). Their lives included brutally hard labor and production quotas set beyond their capabilities. Yet the Hebrew nation prospered. (In Jeremiah 29:7, the Lord says that when the land prospers, His people prosper with it.) The people of Egypt started to fear them. In retaliation, Pharaoh issued an edict to kill all newborn Hebrew boys. But God had a special plan for Moses' life. His hand of intervention would intricately weave together Moses' first years.

List three occurrences that show God's intervening hand in Moses' infancy.

Who were the positive influences God placed in Moses' young life?

5. Continue reading Exodus 2:11–25. As Moses grew up in the Egyptian palace, he witnessed the profound oppression of his people, the Hebrews, and perhaps

he wished he could solve all the injustices. Unfortunately, he tried.

In Exodus 2:11–14, what negative action does Moses take?

What were the immediate consequences from his fellow Hebrews?

From Pharaoh (his adopted grandfather)?

Despite Moses' actions, what positive things did God allow to come from those circumstances?

6. Just as God had a great plan for Moses that unfolded throughout his life, God has a wonderful plan for you. Part of that plan is sharing in a growing relationship with Him here on earth and then a glorious life someday in heaven. Read Romans 8:28 and Ephesians 1:11–12. Then answer the following:

Looking back over your life, what circumstances, like Moses, have you overcome "against all odds"? Upon reflection, can you see God's mighty hand in any of them?

What do the verses above say about how God is working in your life today?

7. Moses had choices. He could have allowed his past sin to keep him from experiencing the positive outcomes God intended from the beginning. He could have felt that his parents abandoned him. He could have allowed bitterness or anger to overtake his emotions, thus blocking any healthy relationship development. Moses could have refused the whole "God thing" based on the suffering he saw all around him. He could have allowed distrust to become his natural response to circumstances. Yet, in the midst of Moses' time in a foreign land, God proved His love for him and His desire to be his Friend.

Are you allowing the hurts and disappointments of the past to block God from your life? Doing so is a choice and a sin. If you are allowing past failures to separate you from God, ask Him now to forgive you and to renew a right spirit within you (Psalm 51:10–12). God will be faithful to grant you the strength needed to endure the pain of your past and to focus instead on His unconditional love and the peace He offers. You may praise God here in prayer for His redeeming love and the continued forgiveness He offers through Jesus. Write your words of confession and thanksgiving here.

Chapter 2

Let's Meet for Coffee

"Then you will call upon Me . . ." Jeremiah 29:12

Have you ever made the call? You know the one. The exciting moment when you realize you have just enough time in your schedule to meet with a friend at the coffee shop for some much-needed girl talk. Maybe you finished running errands sooner than you expected. Maybe the doctor's office called and asked to reschedule your one o'clock appointment. Or maybe another mom called and invited your child to come over to play, leaving you with an hour or two of coveted free time. No matter what the circumstance, you quickly decide that you want to spend this time with a friend, sharing the most recent happenings of your lives.

Can you picture the scene? The time to meet arrives. You see the many small tables filled with people chatting. You smell the caramel macchiatos, the French vanilla lattes, and the strong Colombian roasts all around. The comfy leather chair in the corner of the coffee shop draws you closer. You relax at the thought of such a soothing atmosphere. You cannot wait to bask in the company of your best friend.

As women, we find many reasons to call a friend for coffee. Sometimes, we call out of desperation. We reach a point when we believe we will explode if we do not take time out to share our thoughts with someone who will listen. For me, these are the moments I tell my boys, "Let's go. Put on your shoes. Yes, you may eat all the bagels and muffins you want. Just please let me talk with Miss Friend."

Sometimes, we wish for another opinion on an issue we face. If our friend has already tackled this issue, then she's an even better fit for our coffee talk. At other times, our craving for conversation stems from the need to have some fun. I recently called a friend, after a particularly long day, and asked, "What do you do for fun?" When she could not think of an answer, we decided to meet that evening for a late night latte and diet cola.

While we come together for different reasons at the outset, I believe the real purpose we gather for conversation and coffee is the reward afterward. No matter how you feel at the beginning of the meeting, when it ends, you are renewed, refreshed, and ready to face the rest of the world again. You feel reassured as you share the intricacies of your life with someone who knows you and cares about you. You not only receive a pick-me-up from the coffee, you receive refreshment from your friend.

He Cares about the Details?

Pregnant with my second child and feeling exhausted from my first, I enrolled in a summer Bible study, hoping to find refreshment there. The study was an in-depth look at how Jesus related to His disciples. A new friend I had met at church agreed to attend with me.

During the second or third session, the group leader discussed the joy of recognizing God's involvement in our daily lives. She shared examples of sensing God's direction while reading the Bible. She illustrated how simple circumstances remind her of Jesus' promise to always be with us (Matthew 28:20). She threw out a challenge to us to recognize and acknowledge Jesus more in our own daily lives. I remember leaving that group meeting thinking, *Lord, You may want me to find joy in You more often, but I sure do not see how I can.*

How could I find joy in God when I wrongly believed that He did not care about my small and trivial concerns? I wanted to believe that He did, but my sin of allowing hurt and betrayal to cast shadows on God's love was more comfortable. I was basing my view of God on my human understanding of relationships, not on the truth of God's everlasting love (Jeremiah 31:3). I realized that I needed to confess my faulty thinking, turn away from my sin, and learn more about God's view of me (Acts 3:19–20).

I also continued thinking about the Bible study challenge. I truly wanted to see Jesus working more in my life, to call upon the One who cared about me. But the pain of my past kept those communication lines closed. Before fully trusting Him, I needed to be convinced that God really would be involved in the details of my life, as a good friend would be. So, I did what any girl from the Show-Me State would do, I asked the Lord to show me that He was working in my life, to show me in some way, shape, or form that He was involved. I didn't want to test God. I just desperately wanted to see that He was going to be different from the people in my past. My prayer was the prayer of the father who asked Jesus to heal his demon-possessed son: "I believe; help my unbelief!" (Mark 9:24).

Two days later, my friend LeAnn called and invited me to her house for lunch. Before hanging up the phone, she asked if my pregnancy had caused me to crave certain foods. I laughed as I told her how I had never liked lemon meringue pie, but I was craving it horribly. LeAnn gasped and said, "Kristen, you will not believe this, but last night, for some reason unknown to me, I bought a lemon meringue pie. I have it in the refrigerator right now. We can have it for dessert." I squealed with excitement.

Then I truly realized that through the gesture of a generous and thoughtful hostess, God cared about the intimate details in my life. He had illustrated it perfectly. My heart stirred with delight as I felt a flicker of hope for the beginning of a new friendship with a God who takes my concerns seriously, a God I can call upon with anything, a God I can trust to hold every little detail of my life because He cares about me (1 Peter 5:7; Matthew 6:25–34).

The Only Alternative

Moses, as the new leader of the Hebrew people, had no one else to call upon for guidance or leadership. Sure, he had grown up in the Egyptian palace surrounded by world experts in management, but he could hardly consult them in his current circumstances. He was now the enemy, going against the ruler of the Egyptians. Moses could not access their advice about moving armies and settling disputes. He had only one alternative.

After God called him for service at the burning bush (Exodus 3:10), Moses began a new friendship with Him. Scripture repeatedly shows us how Moses called upon God for answers to his self-doubts and his concerns for the Hebrew nation. While respectful in nature, Moses' conversations with God were earnest and honest. He did not hold back his true thoughts or feelings. Moses believed in God's willingness to handle anything that he felt was worthy of conversation. He trusted in God's power. Time and time again, God proved faithful.

When frustrated or concerned, we may turn to friends, books, the Internet, or television programs for relief and answers. We may find temporary solutions to our aggravations, but how often do these resources provide *lasting* value? Do we find the underlying resolution for which we are looking? Do we truly find someone who understands our needs and us?

What if our only alternative for guidance was conversation and time with the Savior? What if, like Moses, we developed the habit of turning first to God? What if we trusted Him to give us the replies we desperately long to hear? What if we knew in faith that He would respond to our every cry even before we knew what we needed? What if we believed we could find sustenance and renewal in Him?

How Would Our Lives Change?

Precious friend, this is what God wants to do for us. God desires our calls in every and all circumstances. He not only wants to answer, but He also wants lovingly to renew us and sustain us through the gifts of His body and blood in Holy Communion. God will guide us and direct us in all things as we meet with Him. As Psalm 145:17–19 states, "The LORD is righteous in all His ways and kind in all His works. The LORD is near to all who call on Him, to all who call on Him in truth. He fulfills the desire of those who fear Him; He also hears their cry and saves them."

Now, we need to make the decision to meet with Him.

But I Don't Want To . . . Yet

I was not always comfortable with the thought of meeting daily with God. For many years, my life consisted of thinking about Him mostly on Sundays, maybe once a week in a Bible study, and sleepily as I lay down at night. During church, I went through the motions of confessing, praising, praying, forgiving, and receiving. Then I would leave and promptly forget what I had learned about Him. Halfway through a typical week, someone could ask me what the sermon theme was on Sunday, and I would not have an answer. I had no real relationship with Jesus or His Word. Instead, I merely punched my ticket at the prescribed services every Christian should attend and called it good. I had a routine with a church, but not with the One who founded it.

For far too long, many of us have been content with knowing our faith in God would allow us a certain eternity in heaven and stopping there. We struggle with moving beyond the salvation assurance. We hesitate to dive deeper into a relationship with Him. Yet, when we look in the Bible, we see people who were intricately involved with God in all aspects of daily life. They were not content just to meet with Him once a week. We do not read in Scripture, "And Moses met with God only at the morning hour on Sunday." No. People the Bible tells about, people like Moses, Joshua, David, Peter, Mary, and John, dedicated time to speaking and sharing their lives with God and to applying His precepts to all decisions and interactions with others.

During the early months of my trying to meet with God on a daily basis, I confronted the issue of "having too many other things to do." I would see the piles of laundry, the dishes on the counter, the empty pantry waiting to be filled, and would think, *Yes, Lord, I want to be with You, but I have so much to do. How can I afford to spend time with You?* Inevitably, I learned that when I give God my time, everything else gets finished anyway. Or, at least after spending time learning His plans, mine just did not seem as pressing. I was always amazed at how my priorities changed after His eternal perspective adjustment. For me, the temptation of not having enough time to meet with God began to fade.

Another reason I initially struggled with seeking God daily was my stubborn, strong-willed belief in me, myself, and I. After all, I knew I could make it through life on my own. I did not believe that relying on God could help me when my child was crying, my husband was at work, and I was feeling completely unlovable. How could I "fear, love, and trust in God above all things," as Luther encourages in his Small Catechism, when I couldn't seem to put anything before me except me? I had thought all along that I was a good person who obeyed all the Commandments. Yet, I unknowingly had been breaking the First Commandment the whole time: "You shall have no other gods before Me" (Exodus 20:3). I had placed myself in front of God and His will for me. God knew I needed to change.

I also was unwilling to trust someone I did not know completely. I had heard in Sunday School about people being struck down with a plague or killed for disobedience. Who needed that kind of friend? God knew I did. He revealed His true self as I deliberately began to spend more time with Him in His Word.

Refreshment, Anyone?

Just as we seek water to drink every day to revive ourselves physically, we also can choose to receive daily spiritual refreshment from Christ. Psalm 37:4 tells us to "delight yourself in the LORD." When I think about delighting in something, I anticipate it with excitement and energy because I know it will benefit me in some way. I focus all my thoughts toward it as it becomes the center of my attention. It makes me joyful, radiant, and sometimes plain giddy. Can you imagine feeling all this about our precious Savior? How refreshed we might be if we wholeheartedly devoted ourselves to time in His presence. We would face each trial and circumstance with assurance of His love and peace.

The simple truth is that the more time, even just minutes, we spend with God, the more He will increase our desire to know Him. He also will intensify our need to know Him and His Word. Through the work of the Holy Spirit, calling on Him in prayer will become second nature. In the time we give Him, He will be faithful to speak to our hearts. He is trustworthy with our needs. He meets them when we call.

Making Time for Conversation

After reading this chapter, you may be thinking that

spending time daily with God sounds wonderful—in theory—but when you look at your jam-packed schedule, you see no possibility for fitting in one more thing.

Dear friend, I completely understand. When I began this journey of taking time every day to pray and read His Word, I did not think I would continue, due to the extra minutes in my day that it required. I also knew that I am not a morning person and getting up earlier each day was not a likely routine. I wondered, *How can so many women claim to get up first thing every morning to spend their "quiet time" with God, when I can barely get out of bed each morning?* I struggled with wanting to get up, get showered, and meet with God. Most mornings, my snooze button won the battle.

Then, through the wise counsel of a godly woman, I understood that God meets with us whenever we are willing to meet with Him. In our busy lives, we make time to meet with friends, co-workers, and others. We can also choose to make time to be with our Savior.

As Psalm 139 states, God knows when we "sit down" and "rise up." He knows our schedules. He will be faithful to show us the available time. All we need to do is sincerely ask and expect an answer. When I began asking, the Holy Spirit showed me times that I had never even considered. Some of my moments with Him now include standing at the kitchen island while I am waiting for something to cook, waiting in the child-pick-up line at school or while the boys watch a TV show, and as I walk on the treadmill. These may not be traditional "quiet" times because I am physically doing something else, but God knows that at this time in my life, these are the moments that work for me. I can pray anytime, anywhere (Ephesians 6:18; 1 Thessalonians 5:17), or I can meditate on a passage of Scripture or the catechism. He is faithful to reward the time I make to speak with Him. God will do the same for you!

Let's Meet Now

1. This chapter begins with the first words of Jeremiah
   29:12, "Then you will call upon Me." By using the word
   then, God was telling the captives that there would be
   a time when they would finally begin turning to Him.
   The people would realize their need for connection
   with God. During their moments of calling out and
   reaching for Him, they could be sure that God would
   listen.

   God has called each of us. Now, He waits for us to
   begin our side of the conversation. Just as we would
   contact a friend and ask to meet over coffee, God
   desires us to do the same with Him. He is waiting to
   be our one true Friend who always hears our requests,
   praises, confessions, and needs. He graciously gives
   us the gift of prayer so we not only may speak directly
   to Him (Luke 11:2; 1 Thessalonians 5:17) but also
   know that He will answer (Psalm 17:6).

   When is the last time you called and asked God to
   meet with you? What, if anything, is preventing you
   from doing so more often? Write your thoughts here.

2. After Moses' encounter with God at the burning bush
   (Exodus 3, which we will cover in chapter 3), Moses
   spoke regularly with Him. Time and time again, he
   called on God to soften hearts, provide guidance, and
   reassure him. Even as he repeatedly met with Pha-

raoh, Moses continued to cry out to God. He boldly asked for what he needed and begged for what the Israelites wanted.

Note Moses' reactions to the various situations presented in the following verses:

Exodus 5:19–6:1

Exodus 8:10–12

Exodus 8:28–30

Exodus 10:16–18

3. Through each difficult task Moses encountered, he felt comfortable speaking to God. He questioned. He cried. He prayed for others. In all circumstances, he went first to God.

How do you handle difficulties? Who is usually the first person you call on when difficulties arise (husband, friend, mother, pastor, counselor)?

Have you considered going first to God? If not, what could you do to remind yourself to seek God first next time? Ask Him now to help you.

4. God yearns for us to call upon Him as our Friend, Helper, Provider, and Healer. Read the following verses. How does God react when we call upon Him? According to these verses, what does He desire to do for us?

Psalm 116:1–7

Psalm 145:17–19

Isaiah 65:24

Jeremiah 33:2–3

Zephaniah 3:17

Romans 10:11–13

5. Moses met face-to-face with God on Mount Sinai for forty days and forty nights. He went there to obtain a second set of tablets with the Ten Commandments written on them. (He broke the first set in anger. See Exodus 32:19.)

Describe Moses' face after this time with God. (See Exodus 34:29.)

6. Just as Moses' face was radiant from spending time with the holy Lord God, so can yours be. While we are usually not able to spend forty uninterrupted days and nights with God, we are able to meet with Him throughout our hectic days. Meeting with God brings

renewal, refreshment, and most of all, His perspective to our lives. God desires to make your face and life radiant with His glory.

Just as friendships cannot develop without time spent together, we cannot experience renewal with God unless we take time out of our busyness to nurture our relationship with Him. Take time now to ask God what you can do to make room for Him in your daily life. Write two or three ways you can make time for Him.

7. Dear friend, there is one thing I love about meeting with Jesus—I never have to worry about where to go, what to wear, what to do, or what time to be there. God's Word says to call upon Him (Jeremiah 33:3). We can do that in our bed, bathroom, car, child's school, office, the hospital, and so on. Anywhere we are, God is. We are in His presence and know His ears are open.

God spoke to Samuel as he was about to choose to anoint David's brother Eliab as king, rather than David, the shepherd boy. God informed Samuel that "man looks on the outward appearance but the Lord looks on the heart" (1 Samuel 16:7). This means God is not concerned whether our hair is messy or even clean. He does not look at our wardrobe or our makeup. He does not judge us. God simply gazes deeply into our heart and rejoices to see one yearning for Him.

This is what is so wonderful about God: He knows us so intimately that outward circumstances cannot separate our hearts from Him. In Romans 8:38–39, the apostle Paul states, "For I am sure that neither death nor life, nor angels nor rulers, nor things present nor things to come, nor powers, nor height nor depth, nor anything else in all creation, will be able to separate us from the love of God in Christ Jesus our Lord." Loved one, Jesus is always there to meet, intercede, and love you no matter where you are. Thank Him for that now.

Chapter 3

So Good to See You

"and come . . ." Jeremiah 29:12

I will always remember the day I met two sweet ladies at my local coffee shop when I was there researching and writing the outline for this book. I found Gail and Diane there engaging in some conversation and planning. They were working together on a church committee and were getting to know each other better through the process. Gail explained that she thought a working lunch would be the perfect solution for them as they discussed the church's various needs and enjoyed their budding friendship.

On this day, Gail had arrived first and waited outside, knowing Diane would arrive soon. She surveyed the cars in the parking lot and those pulling into it. After a few minutes, and with no Diane in sight, Gail went inside to see if Diane was already waiting for her. With expectancy, she made her way indoors. Again, she scoped out her surroundings, carefully checking each table for Diane. Not finding her, Gail sat down to wait.

Fifteen minutes later, Diane arrived, rushing through the door saying, "Here I am." Gail sprung from her chair and warmly greeted Diane. After learning that nothing was wrong with Diane, she hugged her tightly. Then each began a steady stream of compliments toward the other, "Is that a new purse? I love it." "Your new haircut is so cute." They spoke of how great it was to spend this time together. They ordered lunch and settled in.

After I observed this exchange, I introduced myself and explained why I was there. I commented about how they began their time together praising each other and complimenting some feature they noticed. Both admitted that their compliments were just the beginning of what would become an intimate conversation. The affirmations spoken seemed to open their hearts and enable them to continue pouring their life stories out to each other. Diane and Gail admitted this was something they both treasured, something that started with a simple "Here I am."

I Will Meet You There

I began my friendship with Pamela under very different circumstances. I had registered to attend my first speakers conference in North Carolina. I had never been to this part of the U.S., much less to this type of event. I had been saving money and was willing to make concessions in my travel plans in order to stretch my funds. One compromise I made was to share a room with another attendee. Since I was the only one I knew going to the conference, I would take my chances and see who my roommate would be.

After landing in North Carolina and riding the shuttle to my hotel, I found that I was the first to arrive at our room. I anxiously awaited the arrival of my unknown roommate. My thoughts ran wild. *Would I like her? Would we have anything in common? Would she snore?* I prayed and hoped we could tolerate each other for the weekend. I braced as I heard the key card enter the lock. "Hi, I'm Pamela," she said in the sweetest Carolina drawl I had ever heard. I knew right then and there that I was in for a great time.

Over the course of the weekend conference, Pamela and I bonded as two best friends. We stayed up talking into the wee hours. We shared meals and stories, and most of all, we shared our love for Jesus Christ. We laughed, we cried, we giggled until our sides hurt. We hated to tell each other good-bye, but the bitterness of our farewell was sweetened by the promise to attend the conference the following year, again as roommates.

Throughout the following year, Pamela and I spoke often on the phone, recounting the latest newsworthy events in our lives. We never ended a conversation without planning for the next conference and our reconnecting there. Everything was going to be the same, except for one detail. Instead of riding the shuttle to the hotel, Pamela would pick me up at the airport and drive me to the hotel. We could not wait to see each other again. We wanted to spend every minute we could reconnecting.

On the first day of the conference, I flew to North Carolina, arrived in the terminal, and followed the signs to baggage claim. As I descended the escalator, I saw the biggest smile greeting me. Pamela was waiting, hands outstretched with a big Southern hug and happily saying, "Here I am." The time apart faded as we began another weekend of strengthening our friendship.

Cherished Friendships

These stories illustrate that the experiences of connecting and reconnecting with a friend can be priceless. Friendships are treasures to cherish, appreciate, and nurture. As women, we often put great effort into the friendships that are most important to us. If asked about the importance of friendships, some of us may even say that we could not make it in this world without certain friends.

Yet, as I think about "best" friends, I have to ask, "Do we see our friendship with God in the same way? Do we actively praise Him for the relationship He provides? Do we give our best compliments to Him? Do we connect with God on a daily basis with the same level of enthusiasm and excitement we show our friends? Do we exclaim, 'Here I am'?" You and I may not be able to answer yes to all these questions. However, we can learn much from someone who did.

Here I Am

In the first chapter of Exodus, we find the Israelites in dire need of deliverance from a torturous life of slavery in Egypt. In all God's power and might, He could have struck down Pharaoh and the entire Egyptian forces at once. Instead, God had a plan that involved Moses, a man who had abandoned a comfortable Egyptian life for a new life of labor in Midian. Focusing on his family, Moses spent forty years caring for them and working for his father-in-law, Jethro. I wonder if Moses ever anticipated when he left Egypt that he would be in the very presence of the almighty God.

God knew where Moses would be on the day He called him from a burning bush. In Exodus 3, we find Moses working as a shepherd in the fields of Jethro. He was far from the luxurious, carefree palace life. His work now was hard, long, and sometimes dangerous. Moses' routine most likely included leading sheep to new pastures, looking out for predators or thieves who might harm the sheep, and finding safe places for the sheep to stop and rest. After working this land for so many years, I am sure Moses knew it like the back of his hand. I can only imagine his amazement and fear when he saw a bush engulfed in flames, yet not burning up (Exodus 3:2).

Exodus 3:3–4 states, "And Moses said, 'I will turn aside to see this great sight, why the bush is not burned.' When the Lord saw that he turned aside to see, God called to him out of the bush, 'Moses, Moses!' And he said, 'Here I am.'"

Although afraid and unsure of what this meeting with God would hold, in all his humbleness Moses proclaimed a bold statement, "Here I am." Moses' response is so simple. Yet, when we consider his words, they are the highest praise someone could offer to God. Moses had himself, a wife, and a son. There were no riches from the palace. He owned no flocks or herds. He had no house to sell. Moses could offer only himself for God's purpose—the greatest honor possible.

Offering Praise

The greatest honor we can offer God is ourselves in praise and worship to Him. Psalm 96:4 (NIV) tells us, "For great is the LORD and most worthy of praise." As Moses did, we can willingly give our highest accolades and praise to our best Friend, Jesus.

This may be easier said than done, especially if we are not familiar with who God truly is. Yes, we know *about* what God has done. We know He sent His Son to save us from our sins, but what else do we know about Him? What do we know about the character and attributes of the God we say we believe in? What is praiseworthy about Him?

In the Small Catechism, we learn more about God. We can praise Him because "in His Word God has told us that He is:

> spirit (a personal being without a body);
>
> eternal (without beginning and without end);
>
> unchangeable (immutable);
>
> almighty, all-powerful (omnipotent);
>
> all-knowing (omniscient);
>
> present everywhere (omnipresent);
>
> holy (sinless and hating sin);
>
> just (fair and impartial);
>
> faithful (keeping His promises);
>
> good (kind, desiring our welfare);
>
> merciful (full of pity);
>
> gracious (showing undeserved kindness, forgiving);
>
> love" (Question 93)

We can also praise God for all He has done, is doing, and will do. We can praise God first for "what He has done":

> For by Him all things were created, in heaven and on earth, visible and invisible, whether thrones or dominions or rulers or authorities—all things were created through Him and for Him. And He is before all things, and in Him all things hold together. And He is the head of the body, the church. He is the beginning, the firstborn from the dead, that in everything He might be preeminent. For in Him all the fullness of God was pleased to dwell, and through Him to reconcile to Himself all things, whether on earth or in heaven, making peace by the blood of His cross. (Colossians 1:16–20)

Not only did He create the earth and all that is in it, but more than two thousand years ago, God left heaven and came to earth as a human being—Jesus. The King of the universe did not live in a palace with servants catering to Him. Instead, He chose the humble beginnings of a stable (Luke 2:6–7). Jesus took the life of a carpenter's son, in a family with parents and siblings. He endured every emotion, every pain, and every temptation that we face today—yet He remained sinless (1 Peter 2:22). Jesus breathed every breath while here for the sole purpose of saving us. He could have stayed in heaven, but He did not. Jesus' purpose on earth from the moment of the covenant God spoke to Eve was to overcome our sins through His death on the cross and His victorious resurrection on the third day (1 Timothy 1:15). This is definitely praiseworthy!

We also can praise God for "what He is doing." Every day that we are on earth, God is wooing us with His love in an attempt to draw us deeper into a relationship with Him. Out of His sheer desire to bless us, He gives us the beauty of creation, the love and compassion of others, and so much more. Nothing can separate us from His love (Romans 8:38–39). No one can break His relationship with us because we are sealed with the Holy Spirit (Ephesians 4:30). While guiding us into truth, the Holy Spirit also convicts us of wrongdoing and turns us back to God. He is constantly working in our lives to make us more like Jesus (2 Thessalonians 2:13). This is definitely worthy of praise.

The third area we can praise God for is "what He will do." In accordance with His will, God will achieve His purposes here on earth through us (Ephesians 2:10). We can live confidently each day, knowing that because of His gift of faith, Jesus will one day take us home to live with Him and all other believers in heaven (Philippians 3:20). We will have all the blessings of perfection—no tears, no pain, no temptations, and no struggling whatsoever (Revelation 21:4). There we will spend eternity with our best Friend, Jesus Christ. We will praise Him there forever.

Finally, as the praise song we often refer to as the Common Doxology ("Praise God from Whom All Blessings Flow") proclaims, we can praise the triune God—Father, Son, and Holy Spirit. We can daily thank our heavenly Father for creating us, Jesus the Son for redeeming us, and the Holy Spirit for guiding and changing us. It's that simple.

How Do I Praise God?

Knowing what to praise God for is one thing, and knowing how to thank Him is another. As I began to meet with God more, I wanted to know how to praise Him and talk with Him "correctly." I remember reading books on the "correct" way to approach God. Some resources used an acronym that was supposed to help me remember the order in which to say my daily prayers. However, I was not good at remembering letter sequences, so I could never recall whether I should use CATS or SACS or ACTS. No matter how much I wanted to remember, I couldn't make this prayer process work.

I decided to try something more familiar—talking to God as a friend. For me, speaking to a friend is effortless. My conversations with a friend usually begin when I say something such as, "I am so glad I could talk with you. I love . . ." Then I insert what item or characteristic for which I sincerely want to compliment my friend. Because of my intimate knowledge of my friend, I easily find something to praise.

It is no different with Christ. When we begin to see God as He truly is, not basing our opinions on suppositions but instead on what we know from the Bible to be true, we find so much to love about Him. As we remember the eternal seal of intimacy He placed on us in Baptism, we realize we are His. As we regularly receive Jesus' forgiveness through Holy Communion, we respond to His gift of relationship. As we begin to recognize His direct and loving interaction in our daily lives, we feel more comfortable sharing our thoughts and feelings with Jesus. The more we flood Him with our affections, the more intimate we become with Him.

To experience this intimacy, we simply share our appreciation with God just as we would with our friend. "Through faith in [Christ] we may approach God with freedom and confidence" (Ephesians 3:12 NIV). Rather than thinking we must complicate the conversation with formal "church speak," we can begin in our own way with our own words by telling God our true thoughts and feelings. He always handles them. He knows us intimately; He is never surprised or taken aback by our honesty. He welcomes it.

God also welcomes all prayers, even when words escape us. Through the work of the Holy Spirit, God hears and understands our prayers, even when we do not know what to say. "Likewise the Spirit helps us in our weakness. For we do not know what to pray for as we ought, but the Spirit Himself intercedes for us with groanings too deep for words" (Romans 8:26). No matter what, God loves to hear us praise Him.

Let's Meet Now

1. Jeremiah 29:12 continues with these powerful words: "and come." These words signified the necessity for change in the exiles of Babylon. The people could not just sit and continue in their usual ways. They needed to turn from their selfish ways and to present themselves wholly to God.

   In the same way, when we meet with Jesus, we take the focus off ourselves as we offer our greatest praise in committing ourselves for His purposes. We act selflessly with friends as we offer sincere praise, compliments, and a listening ear. We can present these same things to our Savior in our daily moments with Him.

   How do you sincerely compliment a good friend? What words could you use to selflessly praise Jesus?

2. When we take time to meet with Christ, often our thoughts are so jumbled and our lives so chaotic that we have difficulty knowing where to start. In Psalms, the writers (including Moses) show us wonderful ways to begin our conversation with God. Read the following verses to understand how you can praise God too. Choose your favorites, and try rewriting them in your own words.

Psalm 63:1–5

Psalm 89:1–2

Psalm 90:1–2

Psalm 100

Psalm 103:1–5

Psalm 145:1–2, 5

3. When we begin our time with God by focusing on His unchanging character, our perspective of Him and our perspective of our circumstances change. We can focus our outlook on the positive aspects we see. Even if our lives are full of turmoil and upset, focusing on a great God points us in the right direction—away from ourselves and toward our all-powerful God.

Our challenge is to focus on the unchanging, ever-present love of our Savior rather than on our own feelings and circumstances, which change day to day. Try altering your perspective today by meditating on the solid truth of the following verses:

Deuteronomy 31:6

Nehemiah 9:17

Malachi 3:6

Hebrews 13:8

4. In Isaiah 9:6, the prophet described Jesus before He was even born: "and His name shall be called Wonderful Counselor, Mighty God, Everlasting Father, Prince of Peace."

Imagine if this verse were the words of a girlfriend, sister, or daughter describing her new boyfriend. The explanation might sound like this: "Oh, he is so wonderful. Whenever I need to talk, he listens so intently. Then he responds with such wisdom. He is so strong. You should see everything he can do. What I really love about him is that he cares for me in little ways too. He holds me when I feel down. He rocks me when I need to be calmed. He constantly reassures me he will never leave me or forget me. And he is such a peacemaker. No matter what the situation is, he is constantly helping others work through their difficulties. He offers words of hope and peace to all he meets. He is just so amazing."

Do you see, friend, that this is the description of Jesus? Our Jesus is everything we could ever desire. If this truly were a description of a man, most might say, "He is too good to be true." With Jesus, however, the words are true. He was a man; and He is our true and perfect God.

By using the Isaiah 9 verse above, write your own description of Him now.

5. For Moses, saying, "Here I am" was the first step toward giving his all to his Lord. He received an incredible lifelong friendship with God following that commitment. Communicating with God became a daily reality for him after that point.

Read the following verses to see who else uttered these same words. What was their daily relationship with God?

Genesis 22:1

1 Samuel 3:1–10

Isaiah 6:8

6. Have you ever said the same words, "Here I am," to God? We have opportunities every day to turn ourselves over to God for His purpose as willing participants in the great adventure He leads. Each day, we can praise our Lord and Savior by giving Him exactly what He desires most—us.

Are you willing to give God your highest praise by saying, "Here I am, Lord"? What thoughts and feelings does this idea evoke in you? Write them here.

7. If praising God or saying "Here I am" seems scary or even impossible right now, you are not alone. Many of us do not approach God as a good friend. Instead, we approach Him out of guilt, obligation, or fear. (I know these used to be my reasons for reading devotions, praying, and even going to church.)

Perhaps the problem is that we are not sure with whom we are meeting. We may believe God thinks of us only as no-good sinners, unworthy humans, or far-removed creatures for which He has no time. We may ascribe many characteristics to Him, which, sadly, due to our religious background, childhood experiences, or lack of knowledge, are grossly incorrect. Praising God also may become very difficult when life is not what we want it to be. When experiencing extreme difficulties—illness, depression, divorce, death, unfaithfulness, or unfair circumstances—praise feels like the last words we wish to say.

Dear friend, God knows your feelings. He also knows the circumstances and the outcomes. He has your ultimate good in mind at all times (Jeremiah 29:11; Romans 8:28). The question becomes "Do you believe Him?" In other words, do you believe God is who His Word says He is and will be (Exodus 3:14)? Do you believe He holds you in the palm of His hand and that nothing can snatch you away (John 10:28)? Do you believe you can praise Him despite your feelings and circumstances? Do you believe even if this life is filled with hardship and evil that heaven will offer no more crying or pain (Revelation 21:4)?

My prayer for you is that you will continue to ask God to know Him as He really is—a gracious, compassionate, loving, forgiving, mercy-filled Savior. I truly believe that the more you learn about God, the more your desire to spend time with Him will increase.

Learning more about God's true character and person also will draw you closer to Him (James 4:8). Why not finish this chapter by thanking God for meeting you where you are? Then ask Him to take you where He desires you to go. Step out in faith and say, "Here I am, Lord," and see what happens as you give God your highest form of praise.

Write your prayer here.

Chapter 4

Sorry I Haven't Called More

"and pray to Me . . ." Jeremiah 29:12

Has this ever happened to you? You finish folding that last load of laundry at 10:30 at night and then realize you forgot to return your best friend's phone call? Even in today's world with so many ways to contact people, you rushed through the day without using any of them to connect with her. Sure, you could have sent a quick text message or an e-mail just to say "Hello." You may have even left a voicemail letting her know you were thinking of her. You really want to spend more time together; yet, once again, you allowed other things to get in the way. The demands of the day and the stressors of the moment crowded out thoughts of someone special until it was too late to call. Rather than going to bed refreshed by conversation with your friend, you crawl under the covers with feelings of regret and exhaustion.

Dear sister in Christ, this is sometimes how we approach our time with God. We allow the tasks of the day, the frustrations of the moment, and our distracted thoughts to crowd out any conversation with our best Friend, Jesus. Unlike our other friends, however, God never thinks it's too late to call. He is available twenty-four hours a day, seven days a week.

My Mistake

Beth and I became best friends during our sophomore year of college. While trying to figure out the world of studying, working, and dating, we leaned on each other for support. We spent much of our time together laughing, joking, and enjoying each other's company. Then I started making plans to go away to graduate school.

Around this time, Beth and I began to struggle with our friendship. Because I naively thought that my boyfriend would be a long-term presence in my life, I started spending less time with Beth. Rather than sharing the happenings of the day with her, I saved them for "my man." During the summer before I left for graduate school, I emotionally and physically distanced myself from my best friend. You might guess where I'm going with this. A month after I left to attend graduate school, my relationship with my boyfriend ended, and my friendship with Beth was strained. While we tried to mend the situation, things were not the same as before.

Circumstances changed, and six years later, I moved to the same city in which Beth was living. Beth was now married and had a child. We decided to try to reconcile our friendship. We attempted to get together for dinner and to renew what once was, but my attitude kept getting in the way. Rather than appreciate all her husband did for her, I criticized what he did not. When I spent time with her child, all I could think about was what I did not have. As I saw all the beautiful décor in her house, I wished mine could be half as elegant. Although we had been best friends and had once accepted each other's faults and shortcomings, I doubted that she would tolerate mine. I did not see myself as good enough for her anymore. I even doubted our history as good friends. Because of my thoughts and feelings, I began the distancing process again.

Slowly, but surely, I allowed my doubt, jealousy, envy, and pride to erode my love for my best friend. I quit calling her altogether and stopped nurturing our friendship. I even "forgot" her birthday. I thought I could avoid any confrontation or guilt and just bow out silently from our relationship.

As the months passed, I often prepared myself mentally in case I might run into Beth. I rehearsed all my arguments about how I was right and Beth was wrong. I allowed myself to become hardened and ready to debate any argument thrown my way. I planned to make sure Beth knew my side of the issues. I convinced myself that my perceptions of the situation were true.

Rather than accept the possibility of reconciliation, I chose anger instead. Swallowed up in ugly arrogance, I continued regularly to list in my head all the things I did not like about Beth. I negated anything positive and vowed to myself that our friendship was over. I would not be a part of any renewal efforts. Rather than communicate openly with Beth, I closed myself off in bitterness and fear. I caused our friendship to end.

Talking with God

Friendship for Moses was not always easy either. We learned in the previous chapter that Moses began his friendship with God by simply responding "Here I am" to God's call. However, after verbalizing his commitment to God, Moses became doubtful and filled with fear of the unknown. In Exodus 3:11 and 13, Moses openly questioned his own qualifications and the journey he was to go on. He wondered about what to do, what to say, and who would listen to him.

While questioning his next steps, however, Moses never quit communicating with God. Though experienced in running from problems (Exodus 2:15), Moses made a different choice. Rather than running this time, although he feared and doubted, Moses listened to God's reassurance. With every question that Moses possibly could ask, God reminded Moses that He would be faithful to lead and guide him (Exodus 3:11–4:17). Moses, in his own vulnerability, turned to the one source who could help him. After receiving full assurance, Moses submitted to God's plans (Exodus 4:20).

By speaking with God regularly and receiving His help, Moses was able to understand how God equipped him to do the impossible—lead millions out of Egypt and into freedom. But he had to make a few apologies to God along the way.

Apologies

Good friends are no different. When meeting for coffee, most friends compliment each other and then move on to apologizing. We often apologize for not making time for them. We describe and express regret for our busyness. We may even ask for forgiveness for not returning a call or accidentally deleting an e-mail or text. Whatever the reason, as friends, we make an apology, forgive each other, and continue with what we came to do.

I find that while apologies to friends are often for superficial or minor infractions, they may, in fact, reflect deeper issues. We say that we feel guilty for not making time to call. Underneath this admission, however, may lie many different feelings. We may actually feel guilty for not making the friendship a valued priority. We may experience worry concerning whether we have enough time to devote to a friendship. We may even feel fearful—fearful of not being good enough or of not fitting in with a friend. We may wonder if she will have time for us too.

Whatever the reason, apologies arise out of our need to feel forgiven, our need to mend brokenness whether within us or with someone else. Sometimes, we also apologize out of a need no longer to feel guilty. The difficulty arises, however, when we are unable to let go of our guilt or are unwilling to correct the problematic behavior, even after we have given and received the apologies.

Guilt can affect us positively or negatively. The remorse we feel after committing wrongdoing or omitting right doing can prompt us to positive action. These actions may include apologies, as we've said, but they can also result in making concessions and rebuilding relationships, actions that point to the Holy Spirit working in our lives. However, if the guilt we feel paralyzes us in fear or anxiety and prevents us from reconciliation, we can take a second look at the source.

God's forgiveness removes our sin "as far as the east is from the west" (Psalm 103:12). Romans 8:1 clearly tells us, "There is therefore now no condemnation for those who are in Christ Jesus." God does not give the sentence of ongoing guilt and shame once we have repented. He takes the punishment away and offers us the reassurance of His forgiveness in the Sacrament of Holy Communion. We may receive assurance there. In addition, 1 John 4:18 states, "There is no fear in love, but perfect love casts out fear. For fear has to do with punishment." When we repent, God does not want us to live in fear and shame; He wants us to move on in love.

You may argue that if apologizing to God is that easy, why should we be concerned about sinning at all? Why should we spend time with God when He will forgive us if we don't? What difference does it make? Dear friend, knowing that God forgives us does not give us a license to turn away. Instead, it is a license to admit, submit, and move on with Him.

Admit, Submit, and Move On

When we admit our sinfulness to God, we open an avenue through which forgiveness can flow freely. Confessing our wrongdoings also keeps Satan and his influence at bay. Ephesians 4:27 (NIV) states, "Do not give the devil a foothold." According to Dictionary.com, a foothold is "1. a place or support for the feet; a place where a person may stand or walk securely. 2. a secure position, especially a firm basis for further progress or development." Harboring sin in our minds and hearts gives a firm base for Satan to progress and develop his evil schemes in our lives. On the cross, Jesus forgave all past, present, and future sins. Yet we still need to repent of them in conversation with our Redeemer. In this way, His forgiveness and compassion will fill the footholds of our hearts instead of allowing feelings of anger, hate, bitterness, or envy to linger there.

As we experience God's forgiveness, we also become aware of His unconditional love for us. When we recognize that we daily live with these gifts, submitting to His plan for our lives becomes possible. Just as God did with Moses, He reassures us that our relationship with Him is not about what we can do, but about what God does in and through us. He does not want our doubts to keep us from Him. God takes every part of us—our doubts, our fears, our imperfections, our past mistakes, our failures, and our future uncertainties—and uses every part of our lives for good. In doing so, He grows our eternal friendship with Him (Philippians 1:6).

When we are faithful to admit our wrongdoings and weaknesses and submit to God's will, then we can move on to do even greater things in our lives. Rather than resisting Him or running away in fear, we can go forward, trusting God's power within us. We can move ahead in confidence, trusting our Father to give us everything we need (Philippians 4:19). He desires that we live in full knowledge of His forgiveness so we can trust Him completely without fears, doubts, or concerns about where He is leading us in this life. We can go forth in life knowing that no matter what, His ways are always best (Isaiah 48:17).

Still Doubting

Are you still having a difficult time believing that with all your shortcomings God still wants to be friends with you? Several years ago, I did too. Even after reading about God's love and compassion for me, I still doubted that He would want to be my Friend.

In my sin, I often asked myself, *What do I have to offer anyway?* I've heard other women speak about "feeling led" or "God speaking to her heart." I often looked at these women as "spiritual giants." As I compared myself to them, I confirmed my own thinking that God would never choose a friend like me. Because of my faulty beliefs, I let doubts, guilt, and defeat keep me from seeking more of Him. As time passed, like gradually losing touch with a good friend, I moved far away from the one thing I needed most—Jesus Christ.

After many months on my own, dissatisfied and disconcerted by my sin-imposed separation from my Lord, I tried studying the Bible once more. What I found on that day changed my outlook and my life.

I opened my Bible to John 20:24–31, the story of the resurrected Jesus appearing to Thomas after He had appeared earlier to the rest of the apostles. In these verses, the other apostles informed Thomas about Jesus' appearance to them while they were hiding in an upper room. After hearing this news, Thomas stated, "Unless I see in His hands the mark of the nails, and place my finger into the mark of the nails, and place my hand into His side, I will never believe" (John 20:25). Reading this, I was speechless at the boldness Thomas had in the midst of his doubting. How often and how long did I doubt, like Thomas, that Jesus would want to become visible to me? Hadn't I also used that same deceitful word, *never*, in describing what I thought Jesus felt about me?

As I continued reading, I noticed how Jesus appeared to Thomas, despite his self-assured statement and confident doubts. What stood out to me the most was how Jesus gently told Thomas, "Put your finger here, and see My hands; and put out your hand and place it in My side" (John 20:27). Jesus continued to encourage Thomas: "Do not disbelieve, but believe" (John 20:27).

Isn't Jesus amazing? He did not put down Thomas. He did not humiliate him in front of the others. He did not turn away from Thomas's doubts. Instead, Jesus gently and lovingly stood there and invited Thomas to discover for himself just how real the resurrected Christ was. Thomas found out in that moment that Jesus indeed was alive and real enough to be felt, seen, reached, and touched. Jesus saw Thomas as His own friend, worthy of His forgiveness and love.

Precious friend, Jesus is saying the same to you. Each day, in a gentle, encouraging, loving, and welcoming way, He invites you to feel, see, reach, and touch His presence. He wants you! Will you stop doubting and believe? May you "not disbelieve, but believe."

Let's Meet Now

1. The third instruction given in Jeremiah 29:12 to the Israelites states "and pray to Me." God knew that in order for the exiles to have hope for change, they needed to focus on Him once again. They also had many things for which they needed to repent. Through Jeremiah's letter, God was encouraging the exiles to speak to Him regarding their circumstances, their captors, and their sin. He was directing them to come to Him.

We also can go directly to God regarding our mess-ups and wrongdoings, our sins.

We can honestly and humbly express all our regrets and repent of our sins to God. We can ask for His forgiveness repeatedly. Through our Savior, Jesus, our sins are gone, and our relationship is renewed.

Look up the following Bible verses. What do they say about our sins?

a. Psalm 103:12

b. Isaiah 1:18

2. Moses, after boldly beginning his friendship with God, quickly began doubting God's call to him. Moses also doubted his own qualifications for the job.

Read the verses listed below, and answer the following questions: What was Moses' reaction/question for God? What was the overall theme of God's response?

a. Exodus 3:5–10
Moses:
God:

b. Exodus 3:11–12
Moses:
God:

c. Exodus 3:13–22
Moses:
God:

d. Exodus 4:1–9
Moses:
God:

e. Exodus 4:10–12
Moses:
God:

f. Exodus 4:13–17
(Note in these verses that although God was angry, in His infinite compassion, He once again reassures Moses and lovingly gives Moses what he needs to succeed.)
Moses:
God:

3. Do you see, dear friend, how Moses is no different from you and me? How many times do we begin a new friendship and then doubts creep into our thoughts? "Who am I that she would want me for a friend? What if she is too busy for me? Will she like who I really am? What can I offer her that she does not already have in another friend?"

Just as doubts assail us when we begin a new friendship, so they bombard us when we receive or renew a daily relationship with Christ. We may fear we are unqualified to read the Bible, to understand God's

Word, or even to pray. We may question whether God truly wants a relationship with us, especially if we have previously turned our backs on Him. We also may falsely believe that God would never share His presence with us. Remember, even Thomas, a disciple of Jesus, shared the same thoughts.

Look up the following verses to read reassuring words from God, just like Moses and Thomas received. Write down any encouragement you receive through these verses.

Romans 5:8

Philippians 1:6

Philippians 2:13

Colossians 1:29

1 Thessalonians 5:23–24

Hebrews 12:2

4. As sinful humans, we will never be perfect; any relationship we enter will need to include confession and forgiveness. This is true in marriage, friendships, parent/child relationships, and our relationship to God. God sent His one and only Son to die for us, so we might have forgiveness in Him (John 3:16).

King David, though a man after God's own heart (Acts 13:22), learned the importance of admitting his sins to God after committing adultery with Bathsheba. We can read his prayer in which he asks God for forgiveness and removal of his guilt in Psalm 51.

a. Read Psalm 51. Notice how David begins his prayer. What reassurances about God's character does David have? How does knowing this about God make it easier for us to approach Him with any sin we have committed?

b. When we sin, we may hurt and negatively affect others. While this is true, according to these verses, against whom do we ultimately sin? Have we always been predisposed to sin?

c. What changes does David ask God to make in him? Have you ever wanted the same?

d. Reread verses 16–17. Often we may believe that we need to make up for our wrongdoing with God. We may try to prove ourselves or show how sorry we are by promising to do extra things, if only God will forgive us. After reading these verses, what do you see that God truly desires? Are you willing to give Him this and to allow Him to make changes in you that are pleasing to Him?

5. For some of us, although we know we have forgiveness through Jesus, telling God our faults, our failures, and our sins may seem scary. We may picture only the God who became angry at the Israelites and Moses. For others, confessing our sins directly to God may seem foreign. Because of our faulty perceptions, we may refrain from confessing our sins before God. In doing so, we miss out on the refreshing waters of His forgiveness in our lives. We forfeit our chance to experience His peace and reassurance.

When is the last time you took time to tell God what wrongs you had committed? Are they grudges you continue to hold? Are they small annoyances that have turned into large problems? Are they feelings you have allowed to influence your actions in a negative way?

Why not try fully confessing your sins to God now through prayer? Write your prayer here. Then be still for a few minutes and notice any changes in you or your attitude.

If you are still hesitant, I have a confession of my own to encourage you. While writing this study, I took a break and read a favorite blog of mine. The writer of the blog was starting her own online Bible study. She already had more than 150 women asking to be included. Rather than feeling excitement for her, jealous thoughts immediately filled my head. I stopped right then in tears. I realized while writing about confession and forgiveness, I needed to immediately confess my own ugly thoughts before moving on. God is so good to reassure us repeatedly of His forgiveness. He also is so good to keep me humble and right where I need to be—doing just what I asked you to do.

6. I am amazed at all the times the Israelites rebelled and sinned against God while they were in the desert. I also am comforted knowing they were no better than I, sinning on a daily, even hourly, basis. In Nehemiah 9, the ancestors of the Israelites, after being exiles in Babylon, made a public confession to God. They were truthful about their wrongdoings and sincere in their plea for forgiveness. What strikes me most in this chapter is that in the midst of their confession, they recognized God's continuous compassion and mercy to their forefathers.

   Read Nehemiah 9. To help you focus on God's character and forgiveness, write out the following verses:

   Nehemiah 9:17b

   Nehemiah 9:27b

   Nehemiah 9:28b

   Nehemiah 9:31–32a

Write any thoughts you may have regarding these verses. How do these verses change your perception of God and the privilege to confess our sins directly to Him, even when we sin over and over?

7. Dear friend, I realize this chapter may have been a tough one for you. It sure was for me! Talking about confession and forgiveness is not easy, especially if you have been wronged or hurt.

I could not finish this chapter, however, without admitting the real consequences of refusing to acknowledge wrongdoing. I mentioned in the beginning of the chapter my mistake with Beth. I chose to end our friendship without ever apologizing to her.

To this day, I still miss her and our friendship. I think of Beth and wonder what she might be doing with her children. I remember her birthday, and in my mind, I wish her happiness every year. I often see someone resembling her and wish it were, just so I could say, "I am sorry."

I finally sent her a card in which I apologized for my behavior. I never heard back. I am still saddened that I allowed jealousy, doubts, and bitterness to have such a foothold in my heart. I am so thankful, however, that God forgave me. I pray that she has found forgiveness for me too.

What about you? Do you have someone in your life whom you need to ask for pardon? Why not start asking God for the boldness and the opportunity to do so? If you are not able to apologize in person, try writing a letter. You can decide later whether or not to send it. All God asks for is "a broken and contrite heart" (Psalm 51:17). Give yours to Him here in a written prayer.

Chapter 5

What's Going On . . .
Really Going On?

"and I will hear you." Jeremiah 29:12

Do you know what I love about having a close girlfriend? She never settles for superficial conversations. She always is interested in the nitty-gritty details of my life. She listens attentively and waits to give feedback until she has heard everything. She knows my nonverbal signals and recognizes when a deeper issue is at hand. My friend wants to know the whys and the hows of what occurs at home, at work, and anywhere else I am involved. She wants to hear about my real emotions. She is both sympathetic and empathetic. She cares how every story ends. Best of all, she uses our shared information to help understand the situation at hand and seek solutions. She truly is interested in my life and actively makes it better by being there for me.

A Supportive Friend

Rebecca was grateful she had a friend like this on that dreary November morning. She met Dana for breakfast and soon began a conversation she never planned on having. Rebecca spoke with Dana about how well her life was going. She enjoyed her new job. She was excited about the upcoming holidays and looked forward to spending time with her extended family. But Dana knew Rebecca well enough to know that while she said she was feeling fine, something else lurked beneath Rebecca's words.

Dana finally asked the question that would bring the truth to light: "Rebecca, what's really going on?" Upon hearing these simple words of true friendship, Rebecca's eyes filled with tears. She told her best friend how lately she was crying constantly and how she lacked energy and motivation. Rebecca sobbed as she confided to Dana, "Please pray for me. I don't even know if God cares about me. Maybe I don't even believe in Him anymore."

Dana reached for Rebecca's hand and reassured her that her simple request for prayer to an almighty God revealed her belief in Him still. For the first time in many days, Rebecca felt relief and hope. She hadn't lost her faith after all. Dana's reassurance was exactly what Rebecca needed.

Dana and Rebecca left the restaurant and went to Dana's home, where they continued the conversation. Dana knew a counselor and helped Rebecca arrange to begin seeing her immediately. Rebecca attended her first appointment with her best friend by her side. She later told Dana how her support allowed her to seek help with confidence and hope.

In time, Rebecca worked through the depression she admitted to on that November day. Never did Dana judge Rebecca or put her down. Instead, Dana supported her throughout her treatment and continued to encourage her with words and prayers. Rebecca admits now that she will always be thankful for Dana's willingness to ask her that revealing question, "What's really going on?"

What's Really Going On?

After completing four chapters of this Bible study together, I feel as if I should be the one asking, "What's going on with you? No, what's *really* going on?" How is your daily meeting with God? Has your desire to spend time with Him increased, decreased, or stayed the same? Do you look forward to being alone with your Savior? Are you beginning to see Him as your Friend?

Human friendships require time and work. They require willingness to dive in, sometimes head first, and swim through calm waters as well as riptides and rapids. Developing close friendships necessitates swimming beyond shallow waters as we attempt to grow together in an atmosphere of transparency and authenticity. True friendships occur within the safety of commitment and openness. Intimacy with Jesus calls for the same types of actions.

I wish I could say that our willingness to have a close friendship with Jesus is always constant in our lives. Due to our sinful human nature, however, we sometimes resist His call to intimacy. We may avoid spending time with Him, finding other things more important. We may feel tired and weary, believing we have nothing to give Him. We may even think that closing off communication with Him is the answer when we don't understand or agree with His ways. When this occurs, what can we do?

As stated in chapter 4, we first need to admit our sins. In the same way we apologize to our best friend when we do not connect with her, we also can confess our flawed thoughts and feelings and responses to Jesus. Then, we can freely receive His forgiveness. As 1 John 1:9 reminds us, "If we confess our sins, He is faithful and just to forgive us our sins and to cleanse us from all unrighteousness." We may be certain that despite our shortcomings, our Savior always desires to spend time with us.

In addition to confession, we benefit from the deliberate choice to spend time with Jesus. He is with us whether or not we want to be with Him (Matthew 28:20). We can consciously focus on His presence and His truth, rather than on all the distractions around us. Whatever the circumstance, we can talk with Him honestly and truthfully, knowing we are fully forgiven for our times of apathy and following our diversions. Each time we choose to share ourselves with Jesus, our friendship with Him grows and deepens. Then, we learn the beauty of being in a relationship with Him.

Sweet, precious friend, no matter what currently is happening in your life, God desires to be your best Friend. He wants you to talk to Him. A lack of proper grammar or a deficiency in flowery words does not bother Him. He delights in your praises. God promises He will gently attend to you as you reveal your fears and troubles (Matthew 11:28). Our thoughts and emotions never take Him by surprise. He asks only that we come to Him.

Crying Out to God

After experiencing God's faithful assurance of provision and power, and obtaining permission from his father-in-law, Moses set out on his journey to Egypt (Exodus 4:20). Soon after his arrival, Moses began experiencing extremely difficult circumstances on all sides. First, after meeting with the elders of Israel, Moses was required to go before the ruler of Egypt. There, he and his brother, Aaron, asked for the release of hundreds of thousands of slaves in order to worship God for three days in the desert. Pharaoh not only said no, but he also ordered an increase in the Israelites' workload. Because of this demand, the foremen of the slaves cursed Moses and his brother (Exodus 5).

Next, Moses had to announce to Pharaoh that the Lord would send plagues that would affect all Egyptian people. Moses not only promised the plagues would come, but he also agreed to ask God, on behalf of the Egyptian leader, to remove them each time they occurred. This happened ten times (Exodus 7:14–11:10). The final act of God in Egypt resulted in Pharaoh's release of the Israelites and Moses' leading them away (Exodus 12:29–42). However, leaving Egypt and captivity only increased Moses' need to cry out to God for help. Nothing was easy for Moses, although God instructed him on each occasion.

In each of the circumstances Moses faced with the Israelites, we never read in Exodus that Moses simply prayed, "God bless Aaron, Miriam, and the Israelites." Instead, we read of Moses crying out to God, declaring exactly what he needed at any given moment. We also never read that Moses waited until bedtime to speak with God. Moses spoke to God about everything he encountered throughout each day. He even spent forty solid days and nights with Him.

God gives us these same opportunities to cry out to Him at any moment of any day for our every need . . . if only we do it!

Baring Our Souls

Are you paying attention to the call from your Savior? He *is* calling, inviting you to meet with Him. Jesus wants to meet with you, not because of the right things you have done, but because He offers healing to you. He longs to grant you the forgiveness you so desperately need. He so much wants you to bare your soul so He may fill you with His love and mercy.

Like me, you may wonder about those times when we divulge everything to God, yet still feel so far away from Him. We feel open and vulnerable, struggling to find His direction. We want intimacy with our Creator and assurance of His presence; however, we do not have a pillar of fire or a giant cloud around us confirming His presence. Like the Israelites (Numbers 20:4), we may ask God, "Why did You bring me here?" especially when we cannot see Him or feel His presence at all.

Just as Moses did, we will all experience desert moments throughout our lives (John 16:20). We will question why we are so alone. We will wonder when our circumstances or other people will improve. We will want our lives to be different, to experience relief, and to escape whatever is causing us heartache. We may even believe that sharing ourselves with Jesus makes no difference. Sweet friend, all these thoughts and emotions are normal. However, separating from the one Person we need most is not the answer. Jesus never leaves us during difficult times (Romans 8:38–39). He is ready and willing to listen to our pleas, even when we do not know what to pray (Romans 8:26). His Spirit will intercede with the Father on our behalf, always working for the good of those who love Him (Romans 8:28). And His promises to us are sure (2 Peter 1:3–4).

Below may be one of my most gut-wrenching prayers to God during one of my own desert times. I share it with you not to tell you how you should pray. Instead, I share it to show that God can handle our feelings and thoughts. He wants us to tell Him what really is going on in our lives.

Lord,

I don't know what You want from me or are doing with my life right now. I just know I want to be with You, Abba Daddy. I want to be what You want me to be. I want to serve where You want me to serve. I want to give as You want me to give.

But I am so scared. Others have gone through so many valleys with You. I go back and forth between thinking I haven't been through enough, only to then flip to being scared of what will happen next in my life. Sometimes I sob so hard from fear, it hurts to breathe. Lord, just use me for Your glory.

Hold me so close that I feel Your breath warm me. Hold me so close that I can feel your Spirit touch the innermost parts of my heart. Hold me so near I can feel the swaying of Your arms as they rock me back and forth. Hold me so still that I can hear Your sweet word of forgiveness. Hold me, Lord. Place Your guiding hand upon my life so that I do not have to fear, but instead, can rest in Your presence.

Father, I love You so much. Keep me from striving for perfection and from running in anger and frustration. I am sorry when I do. Help me, hold me until I rest quietly in Your arms.

Thank You for holding my future, my husband, my children, my family, and my friends. Thank You for Your forgiveness. I love You, Lord, more than I have ever loved anything or anyone else. You alone are my rock and salvation. I find hope in You. I pray this in Jesus' precious name. Your will be done.

Amen.

As Moses' experiences show, God does handle our true feelings, even during our most difficult times. Whatever we do, feel, or believe when we are at our worst, we can hold on to Him because He holds us secure in His grace. We can cling to the truth that Jesus is always there, willing and waiting to hear our every word and to listen to our every cry. He will never leave us or forsake us, even if we turn our back on Him for a time. Nothing can separate us from our heavenly Father's love (Romans 8:38–39). He promises that He will be faithful. As 2 Timothy 2:13 states, "If we are faithless, He remains faithful—for He cannot deny Himself."

Let's Meet Now

1. The last portion of Jeremiah 29:12—"and I will hear you"—assures us of God's response to our calling, coming, and praying to Him. What hope this promise must have given to those living away from their homeland! Their God would listen to their cries and pleas for mercy.

   When we meet with close friends for coffee, we often tell them what is occurring in our lives. We may begin with the temporal and less significant items. Inevitably, however, we end up sharing our deepest needs and issues. We trust our friends with our most personal cares.

   God is no different. As our perfect Friend, He desires to know our every thought, feeling, and longing. If you could share anything with Him right now, what would it be? Disclose it to Him in prayer now. He delights in listening to you!

2. After being in the Lord's presence at the burning bush, Moses made a commitment to Him. From that moment on, he worked to obey God, even when the future seemed uncertain. Moses returned to Egypt. With Aaron, he informed Pharaoh of God's demand to release the Hebrews (Exodus 5:1–3). Upon hearing this, Pharaoh reacted in the exact opposite way Moses had hoped, as did the Israelites. Despite this, God was still in control.

a. Read Exodus 5:4–18. What was Pharaoh's reaction and instructions for the Israelites/Hebrew slaves? What did the slave drivers do in response?

b. Now read Exodus 5:19–21. What was the reaction of the supervisors of Israel?

c. Because of this situation, Moses went directly to God with his complaints. See Exodus 5:22–23. What was his complaint?

d. Read Exodus 6:1–8. How did God answer Moses' complaint? What instructions did He ask Moses to carry out?

e. Now read Exodus 6:9. Moses had just reminded the Israelites of the wonderful covenant God promised their ancestors, a promise of being God's chosen people redeemed by Him. Read the verse closely. What was the Israelites' reaction to this promise and why?

f. Finally, read Exodus 6:10–12, 28–30. What was Moses' final reaction to God's instructions for him? Based on what had just occurred, what emotions or thoughts do you think Moses was having at this point?

3. Moses knew God was going to work with a mighty hand, yet the results he expected were not occurring when he wanted them to occur. Rather than getting better immediately, the conditions worsened. In addition, all those around Moses were discouraged and unwilling to listen to anything else he said.

a. When have you gone to God in prayer regarding a situation that did not resolve in the time you wished?

b. Moses was comfortable talking with God frankly and honestly. He was willing to tell God what was truly on his heart and mind. Moses even questioned God and His methods.

What I love about Moses is that throughout his discouragement, he continued to converse with God. Rather than turning away from Him in frustration, he pursued God even harder. He continued to seek God's perspective.

Have you been in a place where you questioned God, His timing, and His methods? Did you continue to pursue God and His answers, or did your emotions cause you to turn away? Do you believe God is big enough to handle your emotions and what's really going on? Write your thoughts here.

c. Note God's response to Moses' anguish in Exodus 7:1–5. Then read Moses' response in verse 6.

God in His goodness reassures Moses that He will follow through with His promises, but not without allowing Moses to endure some hardship. Because he knew the truth of God's promise, Moses obeyed again.

Often in times of despondency, God gives us reassurances too. We will not recognize them, however, if we turn away in frustration or anger or believe God cannot handle our unique needs. When we continue to seek God through prayer and seek answers in His Word, He will give us His eternal perspective on the situation at hand.

Ask God here, today, to give you the desire to continue talking with Him honestly about your own personal circumstances. Know that He will answer in His time and with His wisdom. Spend time looking and listening for reassurances from Him in His Word. (You may want to use a concordance or topical index in your Bible to find specific verses related to your situation. *The Lutheran Study Bible* offers an extensive index for this purpose.)

4. During times of difficulty, God often sends people into our lives to assist us, guide us, and provide for our immediate needs. God sent Moses such helpers. Read the following verses to see how God supplied much needed strength and support for Moses. Write in your own words the type of help given.

   Exodus 17:8–13

   Exodus 18:13–23

   Numbers 11:11–17

5. In the preceding scenarios, God provided needed mentors, leaders, and friends to come alongside Moses to assist him. Dear sweet friend, God provides the same for us today. When our lives become tiresome or burdensome and our faith seems weak, God sends others to hold us up. Someone may offer meals, childcare, adult care, transportation, help in our home, prayer, a listening ear, or a shoulder to lean on. Someone else, a pastor or teacher or friend, may offer spiritual guidance and a Gospel message that comes directly from the Bible. God helps us and guarantees His victory in these ways.

Many times, however, we resist or reject this help, thinking we are not deserving or worthy. Other times, we allow our pride to intervene, believing we should be able to handle things on our own. Then, when alone again, we wonder if God truly cares about our situation and us. Precious daughter of God, He does! Just as God brought hope and help to Moses, He desires to give the same to you. Will you let Him?

Write a prayer of thanksgiving for God's provision. Ask Him to help you see and accept His help from others who may be reaching out and helping you in your life. If you do not have such persons in your life right now, ask God to place them in your path and to give you the support you need.

6. When God sends others alongside of us, we can accept their assistance. What we have to watch, however, is our tendency to talk with them alone and forfeit time with God.

In reading through much of Exodus, you will notice the Israelites' tendency to complain to one another and to Moses. Complaining, while sometimes a stress releaser, is often a stress increaser instead. Moses had the right idea when he repeatedly took his complaints to the only one who could do anything about them—God.

In times of difficulty, we can call on God first, rather than merely complaining to a friend or loved one. If we still need to speak with someone, we will find our perspective and words are much kinder after time with Him. We can always know that when we share our concerns with God, He will be faithful to provide needed help and reassurance.

How do you handle your concerns of stress, anxiety, or unhappiness? Do you find yourself griping and complaining to others about how life is, rather than going to the only true source of help? Make a commitment this week to go to God in prayer before talking with that friend, sister, or spouse.

7. If talking freely with God still seems an impossible task, take heart. You can simply rely on the help of His Holy Spirit (John 15:26–27). Remember, you can talk with your Savior, just as you would talk with a friend over coffee. Talk to God now through a written prayer. You may want to write it in letter form, just as you would in an e-mail or a letter to a friend. God will help you, in His perfect timing and plan.

Chapter 6

Show Me Your Pictures

"You will seek Me and find Me . . ." Jeremiah 29:13

I love looking at photographs, don't you? They spark so much imagining about a person's life and character. One look at someone's eyes or smile can tell you more than a thousand words.

Other people's vacation photos especially intrigue me. The pictures allow me to share in another person's experience and help me to appreciate the places visited. So when my friend Julia and I decided to meet for some girl talk recently, I was thrilled that she was bringing her vacation pictures. I was particularly interested in seeing her photos because my family had just returned from the same location.

We laughed as we arrived, each carrying hundreds of photos. For over an hour, we discussed all the details of our vacations. Using the photos as a reminder of each place visited, we shared the memories that were precious to each of us. Some were serious; some were silly. All were a record of our families' histories. More than once, we commented that we should frame certain photographs to remind our loved ones of the time spent together. After all, we wanted them to cherish those blessed moments too.

Later, as I reflected on my time spent with Julia, I realized that while our vacations had been similar, our experiences were unique. The photos we chose as important revealed our personal stories—stories that would serve as memories for the rest of our lives, stories we could pass on as a family legacy.

Pictures of God's Provision

In the Old Testament, we read Moses' instructions to the Israelites to tell the next generations about God's deeds and faithfulness to them (Exodus 10:2; 12:42; 16:32; Deuteronomy 7:9). From the moment God sent Moses to Egypt to the day Joshua walked them into Canaan, the Israelites witnessed God's mighty hand in their lives.

Why was this request, to tell about these mighty acts, so important to God? Our omniscient God knew that only when the Israelites recounted His provision would they have the context of God's undeniable work in their lives and the confidence to seize that which was promised to them and their ancestors—a land flowing with milk and honey (Exodus 3:17). Only when they shared these verbal pictures would their children understand fully the character of the great I AM, the God whom they worshiped.

Can you imagine being an Israelite parent living in Canaan and describing the stories of your ancestors' wanderings in the wilderness? Can you visualize yourself describing the immense cloud that steadily moved in front of all the hundreds of thousands of people as they traveled by day and the roaring pillar of fire that guided them at night (Exodus 13:21–22)? Picture your children's faces as you tell of the fear and amazement your ancestors may have felt as they walked between two walls of seawater, praying there was no sudden leak (Exodus 14:21–22). How would they react as you explained that the food they ate was provided by God every morning, miraculously appearing just as the sun rose and melting away as the sun crossed the sky (Exodus 16:21)? What would your children say as you reveal how water sprang from a dry rock after Moses walloped it with his staff (Exodus 17:6)? Imagine your children's reactions as you conveyed how Israel defeated a huge army due to two men's willingness to hold up Moses' arms after he could no longer hold them up himself (Exodus 17:12). Teaching moments such as these allowed the Israelites to share pictures of their lives. These were their portraits of God.

In the same way, photographs are reminders of our history and the activities in our lives. They show us what has changed and what has stayed the same. They allow us to see the character of the people in the pictures. They provide reference points for considering the past, current, and expected happenings.

A Personal Picture from God

Recently, I witnessed a beautiful picture of God's faithfulness in the lives of two orphans from Russia. Not only did God work in a big way to assure their adoption into a loving family in our church, but He also orchestrated events no other could have put together.

After arriving in the United States, the children struggled with the language barrier with their new family. While this was going on, our pastor happened to speak with a gentleman about teaching a Bible study for our congregation. During that discussion, the man mentioned that a missionary and his wife, whom they sponsor, had recently returned from Russia. While the couple was there, they had learned the Russian language. As a result of this conversation, our pastor contacted the missionary couple immediately and asked for their assistance. The couple willingly and lovingly helped the adopting family with their needs.

Next, the children's new parents asked about the possibility of having a reaffirmation of Baptism for the Russian children. (Both children had been baptized at their individual orphanages.) The service was approved, but again, the language barrier was an obstacle. Despite this, the family scheduled the reaffirmation, believing God would make a way.

The week of the reaffirmation service arrived. In yet another sequence of events, the head pastor of the denomination's church in Russia "just happened" to be visiting the local seminary. A Russian translator accompanied him. When contacted by our congregation's pastor, the Russian pastor and the translator graciously agreed to perform the rite during the church service. They would conduct it in both Russian and English.

During the service, the children listened and responded in their native language. We, the congregation, understood the liturgy in English, thanks to the translator.

The day was extremely emotional. We all realized that only God could orchestrate the meeting of two countries and the translation of two languages in such a glorifying manner. We were all witnesses of God's faithfulness to His children. Only He could take what once seemed impossible and make it into something so beautiful. It was a reaffirmation of faith for everyone in the service that day.

God's Photo Album

God shows portraits of His faithfulness throughout His Word, the Bible. In order to learn more about Him, to know Him better, we can spend time looking at these pictures. As we open His Word, we may gaze at His precious images.

Although some may believe that in order to understand the Bible we need a theology degree or special training in biblical study, this is simply untrue. God promises that we can simply approach Him with a desire to know Him, and He will reveal Himself to us. James 4:8 states, "Draw near to God, and He will draw near to you."

As we approach God's Word, we will discover the personal truths that God has given to us. His translator, the Holy Spirit, makes this possible. The Holy Spirit dwells within every believer (1 Corinthians 3:16). He reveals truth to our hearts and spirit in words we can understand (John 16:13). He provides explanations of verses that will touch us deep in our inner being (Hebrews 4:12).

The Holy Spirit helps us learn God's truths in a way that is just as unique as we are. The more we read God's Word, the more the Holy Spirit interprets it for us so we can better learn it. As we become familiar with the Bible and all it says, we learn the language of God. The more we study His biblical portraits, the more we will recognize Him and His workings in our lives and in those around us.

Making His Word Relevant

As you read this chapter, you still may be thinking, *But I have tried to read the Bible, and I just do not understand it. The text is too hard to comprehend. The Holy Spirit didn't help me.* Dear friend, I understand. I truly believe that in some form, we all have experienced this same frustration. We all have faced this roadblock.

So, I ask, what helps us take hold of the stories and instructions in God's Word and make them relevant to our life today? How do we better grasp all that the Bible holds?

Let's start by answering this question: When you sit down to read a romance novel, how often do you choose one of Shakespeare's plays? Most of us would respond "never." We choose instead to read a more modern love story that we can easily understand. The book may follow the same plot and sequences of a Shakespeare original, but it is more relevant to us because of the contemporary language used.

Please know that translations of the Bible exist that remain true to the original text but are offered in modern English for today's reader. They are the same Bible you may have tried to read, but the words are easier to understand. Before you make a selection, I recommend seeking the advice and input of your pastor, women's ministry leader, or another trusted believer. Reading selected passages from different translations also may be helpful in understanding the language used.[1]

Sweet friend, I strongly believe that many of us are missing out on the greatest romance ever written because we stand behind the excuse of not understanding the language. If you find yourself saying or thinking this, please step out in faith today and find a Bible translation that is authentic and meaningful to you. We do not need to shut ourselves out due to fear. Our God is big enough to speak to us through different translations of His Word (even in more modern modes of media such as podcasts, eBooks, and audio versions). His Spirit, our Translator, will teach our hearts according to His will.

You also may want to investigate Christian books, commentaries, and other Bible studies that can give you direction in your Bible reading. Many resources focus on God's character, His provision, and His forgiveness. Study topics such as prayer, perseverance, and women's issues are also great starts.

Wherever you begin or continue, I cannot emphasize enough the importance of getting into the Bible. God's Spirit will speak to us and make the Bible relevant and integral to our lives when we willingly expose ourselves regularly to His Word. We will realize that He is always sincere in keeping His promises. What He says, He will do.

---

1   While translations may be a matter of preference, it is important to note that some paraphrased Bibles are not recognized for accuracy. Study Bibles, such as The Lutheran Study Bible from Concordia Publishing House, provide extensive notes, cross references, articles, and commentary specifically to aid today's reader in understanding and applying Scripture to her life.

Let's Meet Now

1. This chapter begins with the first words of Jeremiah 29:13, "You will seek Me and find Me." Jeremiah could write these words in his letter to the exiles, knowing God's promise always to be near those who call upon Him. Generations had passed down stories of God's faithfulness to them and their people. This generation was no different. Because of this history, they could go forward in faith.

   We similarly may share stories and photos with our friends when we meet for coffee. As our Friend, God desires to share His pictures with us through the Bible. As the verse states, however, we must do some seeking of our own. We are the only ones who can make time in our lives to meet with our Savior in His Word and to receive Him in the Sacrament. Unlike other tasks, we cannot delegate this one to others.

   In your life, what do you always seem to be able to make time to do? Notice I said "make time." This is a deliberate action. How easy is it to make time for God? As you work through the chapters in *Coffee with the Savior*, is it becoming easier? Write your thoughts here.

2. During Moses' leadership of the Israelites, God proved His faithfulness in many ways. God promised the people that He not only would bring them out of Egypt, but He would also bring them to the land sworn to their ancestors, Abraham, Isaac, and Jacob (Exodus 6:6–8). While the Israelites experienced delays in reaching the Promised Land, they nevertheless reached it, in God's perfect timing.

Read God's original promise of deliverance in Exodus 3:16–20 and Exodus 6:1–8. Then read the verses below. Note the ways in which God was faithful to His promise for Moses and the Israelites.

Exodus 12:31–37

Exodus 13:21–22

Exodus 14:13–31

Exodus 16:1–18

Exodus 17:3–6

3. God proved faithful in His promises to Moses, the Israelites, and the two precious adopted children mentioned earlier in this chapter. In the same way, He is faithful to each of us. Through the blessings of His Means of Grace, God daily provides us with His deliverance, guidance, provision, and needed help. We need only to stop and recognize His hand in our individual circumstances.

Think of a time recently when you experienced the faithfulness of God. Write about your experience here. Include what God taught you through it.

4. During difficult times in our lives, God's faithfulness may not seem as real as the impending circumstances. Don't you think that Moses sometimes felt the same way? Yet repeatedly, Moses chose to believe God and His promises.

We can learn from Moses. During episodes when our emotions and thoughts seem more real than God, we can turn to His pictures—the Bible. We can read His words of reassurance. Then, we can choose to believe His everlasting promises.

Take time to look up the following verses of truth about God's faithfulness. Try to memorize one or two verses to combat the annoying doubts that come your way. Or write a couple of the verses where you can turn to them when you need to. Then you can choose, minute-by-minute and hour-by-hour as Moses did, to meditate on God's Word, believe it, and stand strong with it.

Psalm 57:10

Psalm 86:15

Psalm 91:4

Psalm 117:2

Lamentations 3:21–23

5. One of my favorite stories in the Bible is the feeding of the five thousand (Matthew 14:13–21). The entire episode is a perfect picture of what Jesus can do in our lives when we are faithful to Him.

The story begins with Jesus preaching to a large crowd of men, women, and children. Dinnertime was quickly approaching. When the disciples were overwhelmed with no provision for the thousands of people present, they offered to send them somewhere else to find food. Instead, Jesus acted on another plan. He first told the disciples to feed them. Then, in an unexpected and miraculous way, Jesus took what was barely enough for a few and fed many.

I am always amazed that Jesus took five loaves of bread and two fish and multiplied them into a feast for more than five thousand, with leftovers. Through His power alone, the small amount, innocently offered by one, ended up blessing many.

I often think this is how Christ works in our growing relationship with Him. Similar to the disciples, we often think that we should go somewhere else to have our needs met. We turn to friends, co-workers, magazines, television, and the Internet for support and answers. We finish our quest feeling unfulfilled and still hungry for answers. If only we would realize that while we are busy pursuing what we think would fill us, Jesus patiently says, "You do not need to go away. Bring what you have to Me."

When we bring what little we have to Jesus, He is faithful to multiply it beyond anything we could ask or imagine (Ephesians 3:20). When we begin willingly to read even a verse of Scripture, He increases our understanding. When we desire to praise Him, He multiplies our thankfulness and awe. When we are willing to give Him all the pieces of our life, to be broken for His glory alone, He leads us faithfully to a place with abundantly more life than we have now.

How does knowing what Jesus is capable of increase your trust in His faithfulness in your life? Write your response here.

6. Only through the power of the Holy Spirit can we begin and maintain our faith in God. Rather than having to make it on our own, we constantly have the presence of His Holy Spirit, guiding and leading us. We are never alone.

Read the following verses regarding the work of God's Holy Spirit in our lives. Describe these works here.

John 14:15–19

John 14:23

John 14:26

John 16:13–15

7. The Bible begins with a picture of His creation and
   includes—after the fall of man into sin—His first
   promise of a Savior. The story continues in the New
   Testament with the birth, death, and the amazing resurrection of that Savior, Jesus Christ. God's Word ends
   with the fulfillment of the promise of Satan's final
   defeat, as written in Revelation. The Scriptures are an
   account, a record, a photo album, if you will.

   To understand this extensive story of God's grace, we
   must look at the entire photo album, from beginning
   to end. If we do not, we will miss the full miracle for
   our lives. When we look at the complete picture, we
   can appreciate all God has done and will do for our
   salvation. We will see that His faithfulness never ends.

   Our individual lives are much the same. God faithfully
   brings us into existence with a greater plan already
   in place (Jeremiah 29:11). He sees the full story and
   purpose of our life.

   Too often, though, we are willing to look only at part

of our life and rule life's entirety as failure. In thinking this way, we rule out the promise of God's faithfulness and deliverance in our lives. We quickly become discouraged, disheartened, and defeated. We may even give up, thinking God's promises were true for other people but not for us.

Beloved, if this is your life so far, please try looking for the rest of the story. God gives you His Word to show that He has a beautiful plan for your life. You can experience the truth of His promises. He will provide deliverance, guidance, and needed help. If you do not feel like God is holding true to His promises here on earth, remember, there is a heaven waiting for you. Like Moses, you will find complete fulfillment of all God's promises there.

Look up the following verses. As you finish this chapter, try using them in a prayer of thanksgiving to our Lord and Savior Jesus Christ for all that He is.

Deuteronomy 7:9

Deuteronomy 31:8

1 Corinthians 10:13

2 Timothy 2:13

Chapter 7

We'll Have to Do This Again

"when you seek Me . . ." Jeremiah 29:13

Our time together is nearing an end. I have enjoyed talking, laughing, and sometimes crying alongside you. I have been amazed at the insights gleaned from Moses' life. I have rejoiced at the newfound friendships we started with Christ. What do you think? What have you enjoyed?

Often, when I realize that time with a friend is almost over, I begin planning for the next get-together. I want to make sure there is no lull in our friendship due to busyness or missed opportunities. I want to meet my friend again soon, to share more wonderful conversation and laughter. Our time together brings me feelings of refreshment, renewal, and peace. I always leave wanting more of the same. When possible, we set another time to get together. This brings reassurance to both of us that we will connect again.

I pray you have the same feelings about your time spent with God and that your desire to meet with Him has increased. I hope that just as you crave time with a friend, you crave intimacy with the Savior of the world. Although this study will come to a close, our time with God never ends. We can seek Him always, no matter where we are or what we are doing, and we can look forward to an eternity in His presence.

Very, Very Soon

Each summer, we arrange for our two boys to spend a week at their grandparents' home. My husband and I drive them halfway, where we meet their grandparents and make the trade. During the drive, the boys are often so excited that they can hardly contain themselves. They discuss all they hope to do and places they hope to visit, all the while spending loads of quality time with their grandma and grandpa.

Afterward, on the trip home, they eagerly recount the adventures they had the previous week. They speak of going to their favorite hotspots, eating their favorite foods, endless hours playing outdoors, and accomplishing everything on their "to do" lists. They talk about their grandparents as if they were their best friends. Even if they miss us during their time away, anything Grandma or Grandpa does makes up for it.

During the most recent trip home, I was aware of a sadness in my five-year-old's facial expressions. Even as his words told of the exciting time, his countenance held something different. I questioned him, and he explained, with tears in his eyes, how upset he was to leave his grandparents after all the fun he experienced. He spoke with longing about visiting them again. From the front seat, I reached back and placed my hand in his. I assured him that his feelings were a good thing that spoke of the connection he had with his grandpa and grandma. I recounted the details of the fun they had experienced. I attempted to make him laugh. Yet in the end, the only comfort for him was my reassuring words—words of promise that he would be able to return to their house "very, very soon."

Wanting to Reconnect

I imagine that Moses felt this same way after spending time with God. He spent precious time face-to-face in the presence of the Creator of the universe, the Lover of us all (Numbers 12:8). No wonder Moses' face glowed from the glory of the Lord (Exodus 34:29). Wouldn't you want to stay and bask in God's presence forever?

Although Moses probably would have loved to do nothing else but sit and talk with the Almighty every day, he could not. Instead, after forty days and nights with the Lord (Exodus 24:18), Moses had to return to his daily life, his duties, and the children of Israel.

We are no different. Many of us would love nothing more than to sit and to drink in God's Word for days on end. To sit uninterrupted in the presence of Jesus sounds heavenly. We may get away on annual retreats or take days off for rejuvenation where we can sit quietly. Then, regrettably, our rest is over much too quickly, and we return to our daily tasks. We must respond to life's demands.

Even during hectic times, though, we find ways to purposefully connect with friends so that busyness does not rob us of our relationships. We desire to spend time together and benefit from it, so we work hard at finding those moments. Sometimes we talk while we are walking. Other times, we pick up breakfast together as we are on our way to an event. We meet for a quick lunch or assist with a task of some kind. In urgent circumstances, we may share time in surgery waiting rooms and prayer chapels. As we do, we prove that our time with a dear friend is not limited to one place or to sporadic get-togethers. We maintain connection.

We can learn from Moses about connecting with God as well. After spending time on the mountain with God, Moses went back to the daily grind (Exodus 34:29–32). He returned to the Israelites and their rebellious ways. Moses knew, however, that despite the difficulties, God was present with him, guiding him behind and before (Exodus 13:21–22). Moses spoke regularly to God through prayer (Exodus 34:34). Because of his needs and continued dialogue with God, Moses learned that he could call upon God in the midst of his everyday life, and his record of this knowledge is preserved for our instruction and comfort. Moses learned it and lived it so we can too.

Because we are God's baptized and redeemed daughters, Jesus is with us daily. We can share conversation with Him anywhere. We are not limited to times at home or church. We can approach Him with the same depth of feeling and degree of honesty as Moses, and we can share much-needed conversation and connection with Him, no matter what the circumstance. God gives us His Word so we may learn and know His ways (John 20:31). We can ask His Holy Spirit to guide us and lead us while accomplishing daily tasks and fulfilling our vocations. Just as Jeremiah 29:13 promises, we can seek Him knowing He will hear us. He will honor our commitment to Him because He is who He is.

The Commitment

A few years ago, I made a new commitment. I began noticing my almost-forty-year-old body was not retaining its vigor and leanness like it once did. Playing freeze tag with my children felt like high-impact aerobics. Clothes were tight in places they did not need to be. I knew that if I wanted to maintain my physical health, then I would have to take care of my body. I needed to make a change.

With encouragement from a good friend, I made a goal to begin walking on the treadmill three times a week and do strength training once a week. But on the day I scheduled my first workout, I almost quit. Doubts assailed me. Who was I to think I could begin a regular exercise routine and stick to it, much less see results from it? I have never exercised regularly in my whole life. Why should I start now?

After fifteen minutes of this kind of self-talk, encouragement from my friend and a few ounces of sheer determination convinced me to get on the treadmill. Those twenty minutes of walking seemed like the longest minutes (besides childbirth!) in my life. I truly spent the entire time staring at the timer as it slowly added the seconds of my effort. I almost gave up and stopped the entire workout at least ten times. Fortunately, my own need to prove myself would not let me.

As the year passed, I continued following my exercise plan, moving toward my goal. I did not stick to it strictly by any means. I experienced days of enthused dedication and days of pure resistance and refusal. Some days I completed the entire workout. Other days I sat and ate chocolate, convincing myself I really did not need to get up and move. I also worked to overcome my biggest obstacle: allowing other things to get in the way of my allotted exercise slot.

Through all the hurdles, I kept trying. With each consecutive workout, I succeeded more than I failed. I began to enjoy the feelings of renewal and increased energy I experienced after exercising. I didn't expect to feel this way, but as time passed I began to enjoy the workouts and even look forward to them. Also, as I persisted, I noticed my stress level decreasing, my calmness increasing, and an overall sense of well-being. Eventually, I realized that I felt disappointed when something caused me to miss exercising, and I looked forward to working out again. I decided I did not want to go back to my previous lifestyle. I was better off with my new devotion to an active life.

Just Imagine

Imagine having these same types of results with regular Bible study and prayer. We could feel renewed and more confident in all aspects of our life. Our stress level could decrease; our peace, joy, and hope could increase. We could look forward to spending daily time with God and miss our moments with Him if something else interfered (Psalm 42:2; 63:7).

Dear friend, I know for a fact that we *can* have this type of relationship; we do not have to imagine it. Our heavenly Father wants this relationship with us and invites us to have it. Our responsibility in making this happen is to make sure our time with God occurs, rather than succumbing to other time absorbers. We are created to be relational. We yearn for connection, so naturally we make time for it. With today's technology, we may speak to others by cell phone, instant messaging, e-mail, blogs, or social media. We have wireless connections and instant updates. It's important that we nurture friendships—but it's easy to lose precious time by repeatedly using these relationship tools.

We choose what is important to us by prioritizing our time every day. We do our part in our relationship with God by committing to meet with Him regularly and knowing that He welcomes us and responds according to His will. Then we trust that the results will occur in His time. Like exercising, we will never do our part perfectly or even close to perfectly. Yet, God honors the time we give Him simply because He is who He is and because He knows the desires of our hearts (Psalm 37:4). We can do this. Believe it!

Let's Meet Now

1. The next portion of Jeremiah 29:13, "when you seek Me," is the basis for this chapter. With these words, God instructs the captives on the conditions of finding Him. God never left the captives while they were in Babylon (Jeremiah 29:4), but they had turned away from Him. God was reminding them of their responsibility in their relationship with Him. After searching their hearts, they were to seek Him in prayers and petitions. This would allow them to walk with Him and live out God's plan for their lives.

When we want to continue a friendship, we also

search for time to devote to that friend. If we stop calling, inviting, and meeting face-to-face, our relationship will suffer. We cannot turn our backs on a friend if we want the friendship to survive.

Unlike relationships between humans, God never forsook the exiles, He never leaves us even if we turn our backs on Him. No matter what, He desires to continue a friendship with us. If we have turned away from Him, whether in part or all, we can repent and return to our best Friend, God. Because our Savior is the "atoning sacrifice for our sins" (1 John 2:2; 4:10), we can confidently walk with Him.

Take time now to seek God and to determine if any part of your life needs recommitting. Or perhaps you have a new commitment you would like to make to Him. Read Psalm 86:5 for reassurance of God's love as you write your commitment here.

2. How wonderful if we constantly yearned for moments to spend with Jesus. We would feel so utterly satisfied in our time with Him that we could only long for more. We would eagerly anticipate speaking and listening to Him and His Word.

a. What about you? Remember the relationship chart in the Introduction of this Bible study (p. 18)? Rate your relationship with Jesus Christ now.

Nonexistent	Seek Him When I Need Something	Meet with Him Somewhat Regularly	Meet Daily	Meet and Listen throughout the Day

b. Have you drawn closer to Jesus? Have you seen an increase in your desire to spend time with Him reading His Word, praying, or just basking in His presence? Write your response here.

3. Life is not predictable and often not easy. Even when we plan to spend time with God, circumstances get in the way. However, if we do some preplanning for times such as this, we can still enjoy moments with Him. How can you prepare to meet with God at different times and places in your life?

a. Make a list of items that you could use while meeting with God (for example, a Bible, journal, pen, 3 × 5 cards).

b. List the places you can put the items. (For example, in my car, I carry a devotional book and a list of prayer needs for my son's school. When sitting in the car waiting to pick him up, the items are readily available. They also remind me to use this time to seek God.)

4. Through the work of the Holy Spirit in your life, you may experience a longing to spend time with God. You may desire to ingest His Word, seek His promises, and experience His glory. When you experience these moments of craving God, be willing to yield yourself to His presence. Even if only for a few moments, amidst daily life, take time and meet with your Creator, Savior, and Lover of your soul. By doing so, you will find refreshment only He can give. In the end, you may find yourself yearning for more time with Him, hoping to do this again.

Read the following verses regarding spending time in God's presence. Try writing one or two verses on a note card. Post them in a place you see often to remind you of His presence throughout your day.

Psalm 34:4–5

Psalm 42:1–2

Psalm 61:4

Psalm 62:1–2

Psalm 63:1, 7–8

Psalm 71:3

Psalm 91:1–2

5. Have you ever heard someone say they put "their heart and soul" into a relationship? When I hear this statement, I think of someone giving every ounce of their desire, love, and self to make that relationship the very best. I visualize people stopping at nothing to make sure their union is a solid fortress in a crazy and chaotic world. When two people engage in this type of relationship, powerful and lasting results occur.

This is what God had in mind when He created us as His daughters and adopted us through Baptism. He desires a relationship so complete that our entire heart and soul and mind will be involved. God instructed Moses about His desire for this type of communion. God made a covenant with the children of Israel, and with their children and grandchildren, to illustrate how He wanted to relate to them. He made a covenant with them, hoping to be their one and only God, the One they sought with all their heart and soul.

Read the following verses regarding God's commands for the children of Israel, His guides for keeping them in right relationship with Him. Write what the people were to do with all "their heart and soul."

Deuteronomy 4:29

Deuteronomy 4:39–40

Deuteronomy 6:5

Deuteronomy 10:12

Deuteronomy 11:1

Deuteronomy 26:16

Deuteronomy 30:2

6. Deuteronomy 4:39 (NIV) states, "Acknowledge and take to heart this day that the Lord is God in heaven above and on the earth below. There is no other." Notice how Moses pointed out in this verse that there is not only head knowledge in believing in the one true God. A person also must "take to heart" that the Lord is God.

This verse reminds us that we cannot only acknowledge in our minds who God is. Even the demons recognize the existence of God (James 2:19). In order to believe and to commune fully with the one true God, we must do more. We must take our belief inward to not only a heart level—a level of love—but to the deepest level of our being, the soul.

The phrase "soul mates" indicates a deep love and affinity between two people. Jesus Christ is our one true "soul mate." It is through the work of the Holy Spirit through the Means of Grace that we have this deep connection of our soul—the relationship with the living God.

How are you relating to the one true God? Do you find yourself seeking, loving, serving, and obeying Him with all your heart and soul? How do you think this affects your desire to meet with Him? Write your thoughts here.

7. After many years of building friendships, I am grateful for the friends who loyally stay by my side. When I take a moment to pause and reflect why these friendships last, I always come back to the same reason. We connect at a deep level. We know each other intimately. We not only have learned each other's idiosyncrasies, but we also accept them as a part of who each other is. We love each other despite letdowns, hurts, and failed expectations. We genuinely love each other as best friends.

Dear friend, God wants this same type of friendship with you. He already knows us deeply and intimately. God the Son gave up His own life so this relationship would be open and eternal. When Jesus died on the cross, the curtain in the ancient temple signifying the separation between the Most Holy Place and the people split forever in two, a supernatural event that symbolized this new covenant relationship with Him (Luke 23:45). Jesus sent His Holy Spirit to each one of us so we would know His presence never leaves us (John 14:16). "For this reason I bow my knees before the Father, from whom every family in heaven and on earth is named, that according to the riches of His glory He may grant you to be strengthened with power through His Spirit in your inner being, so that Christ may dwell in your hearts through faith—that you, being rooted and grounded in love, may have strength to comprehend with all the saints what is the breadth and length and height and depth, and to know the love of Christ that surpasses knowledge, that you may be filled with all the fullness of God" (Ephesians 3:14–19).

Are you willing to settle for merely knowing God as an acquaintance? Or do you desire to know Him as your one true Friend who loves you unconditionally? Are you willing to simply read a daily devotion and call it good? Or do you yearn to meet and hold fast to the one true and living God who sustains and uplifts you?

Sister in Christ, do not settle for less. Just as a good friend accepts you with all your faults, Jesus' death on the cross means that God accepts you for who you are. He loves you that much! He will make you into something you will never achieve on your own. He loves you. He loves you. He loves you. Receive His friendship. Receive communion with Him again and again!

Take a moment now. Write a prayer to God thanking Him for His never-ending friendship. Ask Him to continue helping you to seek and love Him with all your heart and soul. He promises that He will.

Chapter 8

The Next Cup

"with all your heart." Jeremiah 29:13

Have you experienced a best friend moving away? If so, you are familiar with the mixed bag of emotions this brings. You feel joy for your friend and the new adventure on which she is embarking. Yet, selfishly, you also feel saddened and even overwhelmed at the loss you will sustain in your life. While intentions to keep in touch are at a maximum in the beginning, over time they may be reduced to a minimum. A closeness you believed would never end diminishes. How do you handle that?

Concluding a Bible study can be like the end of a friendship. We finish with intentions to continue studying God's Word, only to find ourselves drifting back to the old way of doing things. We intend to continue meeting with God regularly but, somehow, we let the demands of life get in the way. We attempt to get back on track, but the work and discipline required seem too much, and we wait for a better, more convenient time. In the end, we find ourselves frustrated, wondering if we have made any progress at all. We feel guilty because we haven't kept up. Let me assure you that Moses was no different.

Moses Was Not Perfect

For decades, Moses had courageously led the Israelites through the wilderness almost all the way to the Promised Land. He had listened to their complaints, redirected their misguided worship, and helped them overcome enemies. Yet Moses had his own breaking point too.

In Numbers 20:2–13, we read about the Israelites arguing with Moses and Aaron about their lack of water. After meeting with God regarding the situation, God instructed Moses to do two things in front of the gathered Israelites. He was to take his staff with him and then speak to a rock. God promised that if Moses did this, water would gush forth from the rock, just as it had previously (Exodus 17:1–7). This act would supply the drinking needs of the Israelites and their livestock.

At first, Moses did as God asked. He assembled the Israelites. He took his staff with him. Then, in his anger, Moses took the situation into his own hands. He spoke rashly to the Israelites, rather than to the rock. He struck the rock twice with his staff. While water did spring forth, Moses had disobeyed the command of God. He put forth his effort in hitting the rock, rather than merely using his words and relying on God's supernatural power. Because of these actions, God informed Moses that he would not enter Canaan, the Promised Land. This was the consequence of his actions.

Facing the Consequences

After years of wondering about God's punishment of Moses, I finally have a new understanding. The passage in Numbers 20 shows that God's actions toward Moses are relevant to us all. His issuance of a punishment was in no way arbitrary or given in anger. God was following through by giving consequences to Moses' misbehavior because He knew his heart.

God's desire was for Moses and the Israelites to trust in Him and His provision. In this way, God could reveal His love and compassion for the Israelites. God showed His love many times through miracles with Moses. As any human father does, God also expected respect and obedience, a result of their love for Him.

When Moses publicly disobeyed God, he showed disrespect, disobedience, and distrust for the Father of all Israel. His example of sinful behavior could not be left unchecked. If God expected the Israelites to learn trust and obedience through the example of Moses, He could not allow, in His great love and perfect holiness, the Israelites to witness disobedience without consequences. God punished both Moses and Aaron out of His great love for them and for all people. Moses took the punishment as an example for all the Israelites—and for us—to see and learn from. Sin separates us from God and the promised land of heaven.

The example of Moses shows us that no matter how faithful or obedient we are, we cannot achieve perfection on our own. We cannot bridge the gap of separation from God with our own actions. We all need a Savior. Without one, we have to face the consequences of eternal separation from our heavenly Father.

Because of God's great desire for all to be saved (1 Timothy 2:4), He sent Jesus to take the punishment of sin for us. God forgave our disobedience at the cross when Jesus suffered and died for us—God's children, His friends. Because of Jesus' perfect obedience, we can call upon Him and spend eternity with Him, our Friend.

But What about Today?

Do you ever have one of those days when you are not feeling good about yourself? You believe in your heart that no one wants to be around you. Frankly, you are not sure whether you want to be around anyone else. You may think of calling a friend, but instead you reason that she would not want to speak with a crying, self-doubting, miserable girl anyway. Does this sound familiar?

I have days like this following big events, after hours of nonstop parenting, and during those wonderful hormone-influenced days. During these times, I tend to isolate myself both physically and emotionally. Sometimes I shut out others, including friends and family. Sometimes I shut out God and the truths of His promises. I skip my time with Him and venture into something I think will better fill my need—eating, watching television, reading, or shopping.

Oh, how Satan must rejoice on those days! For during these times, his battery of lies easily spirals me deeper into the oblivion of sin. When I choose belief in my own feelings (and hormones) rather than in the truth of God's Word, Satan's lies become even more believable. Almost effortlessly, I doubt my worth, my purpose, and my future. Then, I feel isolated, alone, defeated, and many times, out of control. Sadly, these feelings are the result of choosing to separate myself from God in sin.

Feelings of hopelessness and lack of control are imposed on soldiers and prisoners of war through the tactic of "sensory deprivation." Dictionary.com defines sensory deprivation as "the experimental or natural reduction of environmental stimuli, as by physical isolation or loss of eyesight, often leading to cognitive, perceptual, or behavioral changes, such as disorientation, delusions, or panic." The use of this process easily gives the captor more control over the victim.

For me, staying away from God's Word and His presence is like sensory deprivation. When I separate myself from His wisdom and truth, the world's voices become so much stronger. I can feel disoriented and panicked. I begin to listen to the "not enough" and "never will be" taunts. The spiritual battle with the enemy becomes stronger. I become, in my mind, just another person rather than a redeemed daughter and friend of the King.

While prisoners of war often are forced into this situation, we don't have to be. With the Holy Spirit's help, we can accept fellowship with the living God despite our circumstances. We can read His promises of forgiveness and grace in the Bible. We can receive His gifts of the Sacraments of Baptism and the Lord's Supper. We can choose to call upon our best Friend, Jesus Christ, for some much-needed outside-of-us input. We can choose to meet with Him moment-by-moment for positive perspective change and truth.

What Now?

What about your perspective and your growing friendship with God? Are you excited? Are you motivated? scared? ready?

When I first desired to spend more time with God, I was unsure of what to expect from our friendship. I think that sometimes when we want to strengthen a relationship with someone, we set expectations for ourselves and for the friend. And I believe we do the same in our growing faith walk with Jesus Christ. For instance, in our newfound excitement, we imagine how quickly our faith will grow and how happy we will be. As we read His Word, we plan how quickly we will learn the details of the Bible. We may even determine how we will finally reach the point of being God's "super friend."

All too often, though, our expectations are not met according to our perceived timetable and ideas. We realize that this process is not all about us. Life happens, so we feel challenged in our new trek. When our plan goes awry, we give up. We feel discouraged. Then, we wonder, *What is wrong with me?* Somehow, we start to believe that we were in charge of making our relationship with Christ grow. Over time, we learn that we can only receive and trust the Holy Spirit to do the rest.

Dear friend, we are the same. I still experience these doubts. I have learned that during times of discouragement, I can hang on tightly to two things that help me. The first is a note I posted on my bathroom mirror: "Obey, just for today. Then get up and do it again tomorrow!" The second is Hebrews 12:2a (NIV): "Let us fix our eyes on Jesus, the author and perfecter of our faith." These messages remind me daily that God is indeed in control of my faith walk. I merely have to seek Him and obey. His Holy Spirit will do the rest. I share these with you now so you may feel the comfort of knowing God is truly in control.

Faith Walks Are like Running Marathons, or At Least 5 Ks

My friend Karen has run half-marathons and five kilometer races for several years. She works hard through daily training and discipline. She commits to making sometimes difficult choices with her diet and exercise regimen in order to be in the best physical form to run. In addition, she trains regularly with a coach and a pacer.

Like the rest of us, Karen also runs the spiritual race—choosing a daily friendship with God. In doing both, she has learned that there are many similarities between physical racing and the Christian life. One day, after Karen successfully completed a race, she shared her thoughts with me in the following e-mail:

A friend of mine (a very accomplished, experienced runner—she's much faster and technically better than me!) ran my last race with me as my pacer. It was my best race yet—I scored a "PR" (personal record) and won first place for my age group.

Why did I win that race? First, because I consistently trained. My coach laid out a plan for me, and I followed it. I didn't question my coach's expertise or decisions. I followed what he said to do. Second, on the day of the race, I ran hard. There were many hills and, at times, it was really brutal. I wanted to slow down. I wanted to stop. But the friend who ran with me never stopped encouraging me. I trusted her every word. When she told me a tip, I didn't ask myself, "Does she really mean what she says? How can I know this is the right tip? Should I choose my own way instead of hers?"

When the race was over, I saw so many parallels to my race in my Christian life. How often do I forget the unseen Holy Spirit and His encouragement? My friend Emily encouraged me in the physical race the way the Holy Spirit encourages me in my faith walk and the race I run for the Lord. How often in my faith race, though, do I doubt God's words or, like the serpent in the garden, ask myself, "Did God really say that? Does He really mean that?" I can't believe how totally I trusted in Emily during the 27 minutes and 53 seconds that I ran. I put my whole life in her hands. And she is just a person. Why do I not hand over my life like that to God?

Sweet friend, the friendship you are discovering with God and His precious Son, Jesus Christ, is the same. Through the power of the Holy Spirit, you can hand over your life to Him.

You can continue experiencing His companionship for the rest of your days on earth. You can receive His forgiveness regularly in Holy Communion. He will never leave you or forsake you (Deuteronomy 31:6). He is the author and perfecter of your faith (Hebrews 12:2).

What would you like to do in your life race? Do you desire to continue with His friendship, even when you may feel challenged at the discipline and work it requires? Do you want to entrust yourself to Him, knowing He holds you in the palm of His hand (Isaiah 49:16)?

Why not determine today that your commitment to this friendship will last? With the Holy Spirit's help, you can receive a friendship like Moses had with God, an intimacy so deep that it carried him through even his disobedience. Make the choice today never to go back to being "an acquaintance" who meets with Christ Jesus only on Sundays. Make the choice (as God knew I would) to go to the coffee shop again. Except this time, take your Bible and meet with your best Friend, Jesus. I promise that if you do, you will rejoice at each opportunity to have "the next cup" with Him.

Let's Meet Now

1. This final chapter begins with the last part of Jeremiah 29:13 (in italic): "You will seek Me and find Me, when you seek Me *with all your heart*." Throughout the Bible, we see God's instructions to His people in which He declares through His love that He wants "all" things, "all" people, and "all" our hearts. Beginning with Moses' instructions to the Israelites in Deuteronomy

4:29 and extending to Jesus' instructions in Luke 10:27, God asks us to turn to Him with "all our hearts."

In order to give our all, we can practice giving everything to God daily. Just as we commit to talk with our friends almost every day, we also can make that same commitment to God. As we have learned, relationships grow only with continued transparency and ongoing communication. This includes our friendship with God. He rejoices as we give Him our "all" every day.

What is standing in the way of giving your "all" to God—all your thoughts, all your emotions, all your family, all your future? Take time to reflect seriously on this question. If you still have things hindering you, ask God to remove them and to help you daily "seek first the kingdom of God and His righteousness" (Matthew 6:33). You may want to sign and date it, just as you would a formal contract. Then, you will always have this as a reminder of the day you received or re-received God as your best Friend for life. (If obtaining accountability or making a more formal declaration of your faith would help you, consider enlisting the help of a Christian mentor and/or your pastor.)

2. Many times, I have read the story of God's friend Moses and thought the punishment God gave to Moses was much too harsh. To me, it just seemed

that Moses lost it after hearing the Israelites complain repeatedly year after year. Didn't God understand this response? I wondered—if Moses received this punishment, then what did this mean for me and my disobedience? Record your own thoughts about Moses' disobedience and punishment here.

3. Like Moses, we all respond to God in disobedience. Take a moment now to thank God for His forgiveness for the many wrongs in your life. Thank Jesus for His willingness to lay down His life for *you*, His beloved friend. How does knowing that Jesus gave His all for you affect your desire to have a daily friendship with Him?

4. Do you find yourself wanting to separate yourself from others when you feel stressed or discouraged—like I do? At what times do you isolate yourself from others? from God? Write about those moments as well as what your thoughts and feelings are when you are in these times.

5. The challenge of having "the next cup" in our lives is choosing daily friendship with God over continued isolation in the world. Determine now to prepare for the next time you are tempted to forfeit your daily fellowship with Jesus. Write out the following truths spoken by your Savior. Memorize them or write them on cards to remind you of Jesus' promise to be with you.

John 14:23

John 14:27

John 15:4

John 15:9

John 15:13–15

John 16:27

John 16:33

John 17:25–26

6. Although Moses disobeyed God, Moses' friendship with God and legacy to God's people did not end. Moses' disobedience was only part of his story. Through God's redeeming love, Moses' life became an example of faith and friendship for us all.

God is our Friend despite our downfalls and disobedience. Yes, we may have to face the consequences of our sin, but God forgives us willingly and lovingly. He never leaves us. In fact, He promises to do amazing things through us, His friends. He will give each one of us a legacy of His glory.

Read the following passages, and note how Moses' story continued and how we remember him.

Deuteronomy 34:10–12

Luke 9:28–31

Hebrews 11:23–29

7. Are you ready now to see how friendship with God will change your life? Ask God to show you, during the next weeks, a special verse in His Word to remind you that He is taking care of everything in your life. You may even want to write a prayer asking Him to reveal His presence in your faith walk. Then, get ready for the best Friend and the best friendship you will ever have!

Parting Thoughts

Now that you are finishing this Bible study, you may be wondering, "What's next? How do I go on studying God's Word? Where do I begin?"

When I first began desiring to know God's Word more, I shared the same thoughts. I knew I wanted to do something, but I did not know what. So I prayed, and then I sought out the nearest Christian bookstore and my local library. With assistance from friends at church and bookstore employees, I found books, Bible studies, and devotionals on many different topics. I started by trying one of them and found myself going back for more.

By completing several studies, I learned some lessons quickly. First, most authors (including me) design Bible studies, books, and devotionals with chapters to read consecutively. Unfortunately, on some days, when following this design, the entry for that day did not always match my interests or needs. On some days, I could sense that God wanted to meet me and teach me a lesson in a different part of His Word or in a different chapter of the book I was studying. After struggling for a little while about what to do, I decided to trust God to lead me to where He wanted me to be on each day. I also started keeping several options available as I studied. He has always been faithful to lead me when I listen.

Second, if you look in my pile of Bible study materials, you will find books on the following topics: motherhood; being a godly wife; reinventing self-image according to God's viewpoint; following God's dreams; prayer; obedience; and writing for God. I do not use all of them daily, but the wide array of subjects allows God to lead me where He wants me to be each day. I always sit in amazement each time the Holy Spirit places a desire in my heart to read just what I need. Sometimes, I do not always like what I read because it reveals my sin. However, I know that God both knows my heart and knows what is best for me. I also cling to the fact that the Lord disciplines those He loves (Hebrews 12:6).

Third, after completing a study or devotional, I do not automatically put it away in a bookshelf or closet. (I realize those of you who are organizational fanatics are cringing right now.) Instead, I leave the book out so I can easily see it. Rereading chapters or devotionals is helpful, especially when I have already turned my focus away from the truths they contain. Revisiting insights and Bible verses is invaluable, especially on stressful days.

Finally, I keep several translations of the Bible handy. For me, when language becomes a barrier, enjoyment and learning do not occur. For this reason, if I do not understand a passage, I read verses from several translations until I do. I truly believe that we can choose a version of the Bible that is understandable to us, believing God's Spirit will teach us through it.

With all this in mind, you may want to ask yourself the following questions:

How do I want to continue meeting with God? With what materials do I want to continue my daily cup of coffee with Christ? You may begin today by asking God to grant you continued desire to study His Word and to develop an ongoing friendship with Him. Ask Him to lead you to what He wants to teach you, believing He will. Most of all, cling to and believe His promise to you: "And my God will supply every need of yours according to His riches in glory in Christ Jesus" (Philippians 4:19).

May Jesus Christ become your best Friend. Blessings in all you do.